Think Yourself Rich

USE THE POWER OF YOUR SUBCONSCIOUS MIND TO FIND TRUE WEALTH

Joseph Murphy, Ph.D., D.D.

Revised by **Ian D. McMahan, Ph.D**

PRENTICE HALL PRESS

PRENTICE HALL PRESS
Published by the Penguin Group
Penguin Group (USA) Inc.
375 Hudson Street, New York, New York 10014, USA
Penguin Group (Canada), 90 Eglinton Avenue East, Suite 700, Toronto, Ontario M4P 2Y3, Canada
(a division of Pearson Penguin Canada Inc.)
Penguin Books Ltd., 80 Strand, London WC2R 0RL, England
Penguin Group Ireland, 25 St. Stephen's Green, Dublin 2, Ireland (a division of Penguin Books Ltd.)
Penguin Group (Australia), 250 Camberwell Road, Camberwell, Victoria 3124, Australia
(a division of Pearson Australia Group Pty. Ltd.)
Penguin Books India Pvt. Ltd., 11 Community Centre, Panchsheel Park, New Delhi—110 017, India
Penguin Group (NZ), 67 Apollo Drive, Rosedale, North Shore 0632, New Zealand
(a division of Pearson New Zealand Ltd.)
Penguin Books (South Africa) (Pty.) Ltd., 24 Sturdee Avenue, Rosebank, Johannesburg 2196,
South Africa

Penguin Books Ltd., Registered Offices: 80 Strand, London WC2R 0RL, England

While the author has made every effort to provide accurate telephone numbers and Internet addresses at the time of publication, neither the publisher nor the author assumes any responsibility for errors, or for changes that occur after publication. Further, the publisher does not have any control over and does not assume any responsibility for author or third-party websites or their content.

FIRST EDITION: July 2001

Library of Congress Cataloging-in-Publication Data

Murphy, Joseph 1898–
    Think yourself rich / Joseph Murphy, Ian D. McMahan.
      p. cm.
    Rev. ed. of Miracle power for infinite riches. 1972.
    ISBN 978-0-7352-0223-8
      1. Success. I. McMahan, Ian. II. Murphy, Joseph, 1898– Miracle power for infinite riches.
    III. Title.
BJ1611.M87 2001
299'.93—dc21

                                                                                    2001019053

PRINTED IN THE UNITED STATES OF AMERICA

20 19 18 17 16 15 14

Most Prentice Hall Press books are available at special quantity discounts for bulk purchases for sales promotions, premiums, fund-raising, or educational use. Special books, or book excerpts, can also be created to fit specific needs. For details, write: Special Markets, Penguin Group (USA) Inc., 375 Hudson Street, New York, New York 10014.

How This Book Can Bring Riches to You

Have you ever asked yourself these questions?

- Why is one person very rich and the other poor?

- Why does one person succeed in business while another fails in the same business?

- Why is it that one person prays for wealth and gets no answer and another member of her family prays and gets immediate results?

- Why is it that someone uses affirmations for money and success and becomes poorer and someone else uses the same affirmations and gets marvelous results?

- Why is it that one homeowner tries to sell his home for a year or more with no success and his neighbor sells his home in a few days?

- Why does one person become a great success in sales in a particular territory and another person in the same territory becomes a failure?

- Why is it one person goes up the ladder in her profession while someone else with equal credentials toils and moils all her life without achieving anything worthwhile?

- Why is it that one person has all the money he needs to accomplish his objectives and another can't make ends meet?

- Why is it that so many religious, good, kind people are always short of money and other religious people have all the money they need and use it wisely?

- Why is it that so many atheistic, agnostic, and irreligious people succeed, prosper, become immensely wealthy, and enjoy radiant health while at the same time many good, kind, moral, upright religious people suffer sickness, lack, misery, and poverty?

- Why is it that some give and never receive in return and others give and they receive bountifully?

- Why does one person have a beautiful, luxurious home while another lives in the slums or a dilapidated home?

- Why is it that the rich get richer and the poor get poorer?

- Why is it that one person is happily married and leads a rich life and another is lonely and frustrated?

- Why is it that one person's belief makes him rich and another's belief makes him poor, sick, and a failure in life?

This book answers all these questions in an intensely practical and down-to-earth way. It is intended for those who wish to experience the riches that are all around them. You are here to lead a full and happy life and to have all the money you need to do whatever you want to do, when you want to do it. Money should be circulating freely in your life. There should always be a surplus of it for you.

You can get immediate results by using the laws of your mind in the right way. There are simple, practical techniques and easy-to-do programs in every chapter of this book. They will enable you to put into practice at once the art of living life gloriously, richly, and abundantly. You will find detailed instructions on how to become rich. You will find many examples of men and women in this book who were penniless and down and out, yet who learned to tap the treasure house of their subconscious mind and find their true place in life, thereby attracting all the riches they needed to lead a full, happy, and prosperous life.

In writing the many chapters of this book, I had in mind the sales rep, the teacher, the housewife, the data clerk, the business executive, the clerk behind the counter, the professional, the student, the intern in the hospital, and all those who need money and want money to fulfill their dreams, aspirations, and ambitions in life. For that reason, you will find each chapter rich with many simple and intensely practical techniques for impregnating your subconscious mind. Whenever you impress the idea of wealth the right way on your subconscious, you will experience riches waiting for you on the screen of cosmic space. It is that simple to become wealthy!

All of the many case histories outlined in this book are of men and women who succeeded by using the mental and spiritual laws I describe in detail. I should add that these men and women "belonged" to religions of all known kinds, and some were convinced atheists or agnostics who had no religious affiliations of any kind. Yet, by applying the impersonal powerful forces outlined in this book, they prospered in a magnificent way. They became transformed men and women and enjoyed their wealth for true richer living.

These people also came from every income bracket and every social level. What they have in common is that they achieved their desired goals in life by using the powers of their subconscious mind in the right way. They are therefore destined to go forth conquering every obstacle to acquiring unlimited wealth.

Unique Features of This Book

You will be amazed at this book's down-to-earth practicality. You are presented with simple, usable formulas and techniques that anyone can apply. The special features of this book will enlighten and appeal to you. They will show you why so often people get the opposite of what they prayed for and will explain how to avoid the trap they fell into.

The age-old cry is, "Why have I prayed and prayed and yet I receive no answer?" In this book, you will find the answer to this common complaint. The many simple programs, formulas, and techniques for impregnating your subconscious mind and getting the right answers make this an extraordinarily valuable book in extracting from the treasure house of eternity within you all the riches you need—spiritual, mental, material, and financial. These will enable you to lead a full, happy, rich, and joyous life. *God gave you richly all things to enjoy* (I Timothy 6:17).

Some Highlights of This Book

The following are just some of the many highlights of this book:

- How a young widow avoided disaster and achieved security.

- How a banker quit a lifelong unhealthy habit.

- How a father's lack of understanding drove his daughter to starve herself.

- How faith healing failed—and cured—a man with severe arthritis.

- How a minister learned a true understanding of wealth.

- How a teacher inspired his students to outstanding success.

- How an unemployed professional discovered the job of his dreams.

- How a poor Mexican boy acquired a great psychic gift.

- How a girl achieved her dream of a visit to a great shrine.

There is a simple, practical, logical, and scientific way that always works for you to have all the good things of life. I want to say positively, definitely, unquestionably, and decisively that by using the instructions in this book, you will achieve the rich, happy, and successful life that you want for yourself.

Let this book guide you. Go over it again and again, do exactly as it says, and you will open the door to fabulous riches waiting for you. A nobler, finer, and more satisfying life can be yours. From this page onward, let us go forward in the light of true workable knowledge until the day you have longed for arrives and all the shadows of fear and failure flee. Then, miracle of miracles, you find yourself the wealthy person you have always wanted to be.

Joseph Murphy

Contents

The Secret of Miracle Power for Infinite Riches

It is your God-given birthright to be rich. You are here to express the fullness of life in every way. Your secret purpose on earth is to lead a happy, joyous, and glorious life—the life more abundant. Infinite riches are all around you. The treasure house of infinity is not to be found in a bank vault or a pirate's trove. It is within your own subconscious depths. Begin now to extract from that marvelous gold mine within you everything you need—money, friends, a lovely home, beauty, companionship, and all the blessings of life. Whatever you need, whatever you want, you can bring it forth when you learn to apply the proper technique.

Dave Howe, an old friend of mine, told me the story of two men, Peter R. and Steve G., who grew up in the same town and went to the same college to become geologists. After graduation, they took jobs with rival mineral exploration companies in the western United States. Peter put much time and energy into learning how to tap the mind's treasure house within him. Steve did not. He was a thorough skeptic about the powers of his own mind. Instead, he put all his faith in the techniques and electronic instruments his professors had taught him to use. He relied on externals, such as physical appearances, conditions, and the general topography of the soil. Early in his career, Steve was assigned to do a geological exploration of a certain area in Utah. He used all the most modern equipment of his profession and did everything he was supposed to do, but he found nothing. After three weeks, he gave up.

Later that year, Peter conducted a survey of the same area. Within three days, he uncovered evidence that led to the discovery of a rich vein of uranium ore. His confidence in the guiding principle of his subconscious led him straight to the hidden wealth. The real riches were not concealed underground; they were openly evident in his mental orientation.

The Greatest Secret in the World

Scientists recently achieved the breathtaking feat of decoding the human genome. The program for life itself is said to now be within reach. One expert after another has proclaimed this the greatest secret being unfolded today. They tell us that in coming years science will be able to alter our specie's basic genes. If we choose, we can bring into being as many Einsteins, Beethovens, or Michelangelos as we like.

These experts fail to understand a vital fact. Human beings are more than their bodies, their hereditary characteristics, their family tree, the color of their skin, hair, and eyes. The Living Spirit-God is within humankind. The human subconscious is part of the Eternal, which does not change. It is the same yesterday, today, and forever. We can be transformed in only one way, and that is by the transformation of our minds. *Be ye transformed by the renewing of your mind* (Romans 12:2).

The greatest secret in the world is that the Kingdom of God is within us. Infinite intelligence, boundless wisdom, infinite power, infinite love, and the answer to every problem under the sun are locked within our own subconscious minds.

People search for the greatest secret in the world everywhere but within themselves. Yet the secret has always been within reach of all. Begin now to tap these tremendous powers within you, and you will start to lead a full and happy life based on *God, who giveth us richly all things to enjoy* (I Timothy 6:17). *I am come that they might have life, and that they might have it more abundantly* (John 10:10).

Your Right to Be Rich

It is normal and natural for you to want to achieve success, recognition, and prosperity in your life. You ought to have all the money you need to do what you want to do, when you want to do it. There is no virtue in poverty. Poverty is a mental disease that should, and *could,* be abolished from the face of the earth. Just as wealth is a state of mind, likewise poverty is a state of mind. If we want to eradicate all the slums in the world, we must first wipe out the mental slums created in people's minds by their belief in poverty and lack.

During my many years of private counseling, as well as when talking with people following my lectures around the world, I constantly hear the same comment from people: "The only thing holding me back is my lack of money. There is nothing that $50,000 or $100,000 would not cure in my life." What these people fail to realize is that their own focus on what they lack is *creating* their poverty. Wealth, like poverty, is really a pattern of thoughts and images in the mind. If these people were to follow the techniques explained in this book and begin to use their subconscious minds, wealth would flow to them in avalanches of abundance.

It is the right of you and your family to have healthy, nourishing food, good clothes, a comfortable home, and the money you need to buy the good things of life. You need the time every day for meditation, prayer, relaxation, recreation, and places that make these necessities possible. The true meaning of prosperity does not lie in having more things. It means that you begin to advance mentally, spiritually, and intellectually, as well as socially and financially.

How She Discovered the Riches of Her Subconscious

I was consulted by a woman, Bettina W., who told me she had been the victim of a series of misfortunes. After a bitter divorce that left her in charge of two preschool children, her former husband moved across country and stopped paying child support. She owned a home, but she was carrying both a first and second mortgage. Her one credit card was near its limit. She had a regular job and also did after hours work, but all the money that came in went out again immediately. It was a constant struggle simply to put food on the table. Bettina stayed awake nights wondering what she would do if she or one of the kids fell sick. As she put it, her life was a total mess.

I explained to her that the infinite intelligence within her subconscious could reveal to her everything she needed to know at all times. She could receive inspiration, guidance, new creative ideas, and a solution to her financial problems. I added that once she developed the ability to use her subconscious correctly, it would also provide all the money she needed. She would experience financial freedom beyond her fondest dreams.

To put this process into motion, I offered Bettina two abstract ideas: wealth and success. As we talked, she came to understand that wealth is everywhere. Like all of us, she was born to succeed, to win in the game of life, because once tapped, the infinite power within her cannot fail. At my suggestion, she began a program of spiritual exercises. Every night, before going to sleep, she set aside a quiet time in which she repeated slowly, feelingly, and with deep understanding: "Wealth, success. Wealth, success." She realized that whatever she impressed on her subconscious would be magnified and multiplied on the screen of space. Just prior to sleep, our subconscious is particularly sensitive to whatever conscious thoughts we entertain. By focusing her consciousness on these two concepts, "Wealth, success," Bettina began to activate and release the latent powers of her subconscious.

How Her Subconscious Responded

When used right, the subconscious never fails. Once appealed to, it meets our needs in unforeseen ways, regardless of circumstances. Bettina succeeded in putting away thoughts of poverty and stress while she concentrated on wealth and success. One night, as she was in the middle of this exercise, her eye fell on a vase she had inherited from her mother's older sister. The next day, on an impulse, she posted a description of the vase on an Internet auction site. Within days, connoisseurs who recognized its rarity had bid the price up to over $7,000.

Bettina soon became a regular at yard sales and estate auctions. If a particular item caught her eye, she bought it, then offered it at auction on the Internet. Within three months, her profits from buying and selling antiques and collectibles were so great that she was able to quit her regular job and do the buying and selling full time. Friends and competitors told her that she owed her success to a "knack." She knew better. She realized that her subconscious was the connecting link that united her with the treasure house of infinity. The Infinite intelligence within your subconscious can do *for* you only when it can do *through* you. Your thoughts and feelings control your destiny. Because Bettina learned to place her faith in the unfailing power of her subconscious, she will never again find herself in material or spiritual need.

The Secret of Riches and Promotion Was Within Him

Ralph S. was a gifted young attorney who had lost several cases in a row. He became gloomy, despondent, and full of self-criticism and self-condemnation. Soon he began to suffer some serious financial reverses and drifted deeper and deeper into debt. After one of the senior partners at his firm gave him a friendly warning that his career was in danger, he came to me for help.

After hearing his story, I explained a basic, if often overlooked, fact. Our thoughts are *creative*. That is, what we think tends to change, even to create, reality. The conditions, circumstances, events, and experiences we go through are not accidents. They accurately reflect our habitual thinking and imagery. I told Ralph that if he dwelled constantly on limitation and lack, he would inevitably *experience* limitation and lack.

In the same way, however, thoughts of peace, success, prosperity, right action, and abundance, if sustained regularly and systematically, reproduce themselves after their kind. We do not reap grapes from thorns or figs from thistles. The law is that we are what we think all day long. Moreover, thoughts you originate feelingly and knowingly are especially effective. Used properly, they will create for you whatever you wish to experience from this day forward.

My goal was to help Ralph begin to make use of the miraculous power of his mind. I laid out a program for him to follow that would remind him frequently of the riches of the Infinite within his subconscious mind. Accordingly, I gave him the following prayer technique. Three or four times every day, he took himself to some place where he could be undisturbed. After putting himself in a relaxed state, he affirmed slowly, quietly, and feelingly as follows:

> Today is God's day. I choose harmony, success, prosperity, abundance, security, and Divine right action. Infinite Intelligence reveals to me better ways to give greater service. I am a mental and spiritual magnet, irresistibly attracting to me men and women who are blessed, comforted, and satisfied with my counsel and decisions on their behalf. I am Divinely guided all day long, and whatever I do will prosper. Divine justice and Divine law and order govern all my undertakings, and whatever I begin will result in success. I know the law of my mind, and I am fully aware that all these truths I am reiterating are now sinking into my subconscious mind, and they will come forth after their kind. It is wonderful.

He made it a special point never to deny what he affirmed. When thoughts of lack, fear, or self-criticism tried to intrude, he would immediately reverse them by affirming: *The Lord is my shepherd. I shall not want* (Psalm 23:1).

A few years have passed by. Today Ralph S. is a highly respected partner in his law firm, and his name is often mentioned as a likely prospect for a judgeship. When your thoughts are God's thoughts, God's power is with your thoughts of good.

The Riches of the Listening Ear and Understanding Heart

I have carefully saved a wonderful letter I received from a woman named Serena W., who listened every morning to my radio program. She told me that her husband, Robert, had died a few months earlier of a heart attack. He was only 38. They had often talked about buying life insurance, but the premiums were high. Money was tight, and there didn't seem to be any rush. As a result, she found herself a young widow with a 10-year-old son, few marketable skills, a heavily mortgaged house, and practically nothing in the bank. She had to borrow from her best friend to pay her husband's funeral expenses. Disaster seemed only days or weeks away.

She wrote: "I heard you quote from the Bible: *But my God shall supply all your needs according to his riches in glory* (Philippians 4:19). The words seemed to burn their way into my heart. Then you elaborated on this. You told us that if we tune in on the Infinite within us, if we believe in our hearts, then no matter what we really need to bless us, comfort us, provide for us, or inspire us, the Divine presence would respond. It is written: *Before they call, I will answer; and while they are yet speaking, I will hear* (Isaiah 65:24).

"I sat down and began to think of God supplying my needs. I became convinced that He was hearing me as I prayed. A great sense of peace and harmony came over me.

About two hours later, I got a phone call from my brother-in-law, Milt, in Seattle. Milt is a software engineer who has been very successful. He and my husband were close as children, but they weren't in touch that much in recent years. I think Robert felt a little ashamed that he had not done as well in his career.

"Milt told me he felt devastated by the loss of his brother, and guilty as well. He had often thought about spending more time with us, but he had been so busy in his work that he never felt able to. Now it was too late. He went on to say that he knew Robert and I had not been in the greatest financial shape and he wanted to help. He was arranging to transfer a block of stock in his company to me. The dividends would be enough to cover our basic expenses. He was also setting up a trust to pay for my son's education. He promised that we would never be in want. All he asked in return was that we stay in touch and visit him from time to time. He did not want to make the same mistake with his nephew—my son—that he had made with his brother."

How a Salesman Hit the Jackpot

A real estate salesman named Rick R. attended my lectures on Sunday mornings and listened to my radio program regularly. He told me that he had been drawn into speculating on the stock market and gotten himself deeply in debt. He had counted on his income from commissions to pull him through, but in fact he had not made a sale of a home or property in several months.

As we talked, I began to see what his real problem was. He was obsessed with envious, jealous, and critical thoughts about his colleagues who were making many more sales than he was. He claimed that everything about them disturbed him. He deplored their sales techniques, their professionalism, their vocabulary, even the ways they dressed. He went so far as to tell me that their success was proof of their mediocrity.

As we talked, I tried to show Rick that the jealousy and envy he was generating reflected back on him. By minimizing the success of others, he was giving his own subconscious mind the message that success is bad, that it is something to be avoided, and his subconscious was responding accordingly. His own obsessive thoughts attracted lacks, limitations, and miseries to him. What we wish and think for others, we tend to manifest in our own experience, because each of us is the only thinker in our individual universe. We are totally responsible for the way we think about others as well as about ourselves.

Once Rick realized the trap he had fallen into and accepted responsibility for his own thoughts and wishes, he worked at reversing his attitude. Gradually, he began to wish for all his colleagues the same success, achievement, wealth, and blessings that he wished for himself. He taught himself to meditate several times daily upon the following prayer:

"I am a child of the Infinite, and His riches flow to me freely, joyously, and endlessly. I am enriched in all ways with happiness, peace, wealth, success, and outstanding sales. I am now stirring up the riches of my deeper mind, and rich results follow. I know I shall reap what I sow, for it is written: *Thou shalt also decree a thing, and it shall be established unto thee; and the light shall shine upon thy ways:* (Job 22:28)."

The change in Rick's attitude manifested in his relations with the others in his firm. They started to see him as an inspiration and a source of advice and support. Today he is in charge of his firm's most productive branch and is often called on to lead workshops for the sales force. He has a solid reputation for his ability to teach others how to sell wisely, judiciously, and constructively. The Book of Proverbs says: *Poverty and shame shall be to him that refuseth instruction* (Proverbs 13:18).

MEDITATION FOR REALIZING THE ABUNDANT LIFE

Repeat the following meditation to help solve your problems for abundant living:

> I know that to prosper means to grow spiritually in every dimension. God is prospering me now in mind, body, and affairs. God's ideas constantly unfold within me, bringing to me health, wealth, and perfect Divine expression.

I thrill inwardly as I feel the life of God vitalizing every atom of my being. I know that God's life is animating, sustaining, and strengthening me now. I am now expressing a perfect, radiant body full of vitality, energy, and power.

My business or profession is a Divine activity. Since it is God's business, it is successful and prosperous. I imagine and feel an inner wholeness functioning through my body, mind, and affairs. I give thanks and rejoice in the abundant life.

⌒ CHAPTER POINTS TO REMEMBER ⌒

1. You are here to lead the abundant life, a life full of happiness, joy, health, and rich living. Begin now to release the riches of the treasure house within you.

2. The real riches are within your subconscious mind. A geologist who believed in the guiding principle of his subconscious mind found the treasure in the earth quickly and easily; his rival, who lacked the faith, explored the same area for weeks and found nothing.

3. The greatest secret in all the world is that God dwells in humans. The average person looks everywhere but within himself or herself for wealth, success, happiness, and abundance. God is the Life-Principle, the Infinite Intelligence, and the Infinite Power within us, available instantly to all people through the medium of their thought.

4. Poverty is a disease of the mind. Belief in poverty and lack produce lack and limitation. Wealth is state of mind. Believe in the law of riches, and you shall receive. Before we will ultimately banish the slums and poverty, we must first banish the slums and false beliefs in the mind of people.

5. You can tap the riches of your subconscious by claiming guidance, abundance, wealth, security, and right action. Make a habit of meditating on these truths and your subconscious will respond accordingly.

6. If you lull yourself to sleep every night with two ideas, wealth and success, knowing that by repeating them you are activating the latent powers of your deeper mind, you will be compelled to express wealth and success.

7. Infinite Intelligence in your subconscious can only do for you what it can do through you. Your thought and feeling control your destiny.

8. When you believe that the nature of the Infinite Intelligence in your subconscious mind is to respond to the nature of your request, the answers will always come to you and in ways you do not know of.

9. Your thoughts are creative. Each thought tends to manifest itself in your life. Thoughts of promotion, riches, expansion, and achievement, provided you do not deny them subsequently, come forth after their kind. You promote yourself. You answer your own prayer because it is done unto you as you believe.

10. Be careful when you affirm wealth, success, right action, and promotion that you do not subsequently deny what you affirm. That would be like mixing an acid with an alkali, and you would get an inert substance. In other words, stop neutralizing your good. Thoughts are things.

What you feel you attract, and what you imagine you become.

11. Be sure that you are not envious or jealous of the success, riches, and wealth of others. Remember, your thought is creative. If you are envious or critical of those who have amassed wealth and honors, you will impoverish yourself along all lines. What you wish for others, you tend to create in your own experience.

12. Whatever you really feel to be true, and so decree in your life, will definitely come to pass. Decree riches, health, beauty, security, and right action. *Thou shalt also decree a thing, and it shall be established unto thee; and the light shall shine upon thy ways* (Job 22:28).

13. Use the meditation at the end of the chapter to realize a more abundant life.

2

How to Tap the Miracle Power at Once That Makes You Rich

The Bible says: *If thou canst believe, all things are possible to him that believeth* (Mark 9:23).

To believe is to accept something as true. It is to make alive the truths of God by feeling the reality of them in your heart. This is much more than a conscious or theoretical assent; it means that you must feel the truth of what you affirm in your heart.

It is belief in people's minds that determines the difference between success and failure, health and sickness, happiness and unhappiness, wealth and poverty. Wealth is a state of mind, just as poverty is a state of mind. You are truly rich when you are acquainted with the Infinite Presence and Power within you that people call God. You are truly rich when you know that your thought is creative, that what you feel you attract, and that what you imagine you become. You are rich when you know the creative process of your mind, which is that whatever you impress on your subconscious mind will be projected on the screen of space as form, function, experience, and events.

How She Discovered the Riches Within

A young graphic designer, Sophie C., came up to me after a lecture. She looked and sounded upset, even angry. "I am completely blocked on a major project," she burst out. "If I blow it, my whole career could go down the tubes. I have been praying continually for help in overcoming my problem, just the way you said. But it hasn't helped a bit. If anything, I'm in worse shape. What's the matter with your technique? Why doesn't it work the way it's supposed to?"

"Sophie," I began. "Let's say you are at your computer, working hard on your project. Would it help if your boss stood behind you every minute making suggestions?"

"Of course not," she replied. "I couldn't work that way."

"Not even if they were good suggestions?" I continued.

"Not even then," she said. "The best thing she can do is make sure I know what I have to accomplish, then give me the space I need to do it. If you're always jiggling my elbow, I'm bound to goof up. That is so obvious!"

"I agree," I said. "And it's exactly the same with your subconscious. By praying continually, you're hovering next to your subconscious, giving it one suggestion after another and keeping it from getting on with its work. What you really impress on it is anxiety and doubt about its ability to accomplish the task you've set. Visualize the outcome you desire, as feelingly and completely as possible, then leave the job of bringing it about to the Infinite Intelligence of your subconscious mind."

"I think I see what you mean," Sophie said slowly. "But I've gotten so much in the habit of praying for help. I guess I thought the more I prayed, the stronger the effect. How do I break the habit?"

"There's a powerful way to break such a fixation spell," I replied. "You should start to unleash the spiritual riches within yourself by setting aside one or two moments during the day to pray for someone else who has serious problems. It might be a friend, a neighbor, a business associate, or even someone you've heard about on TV. The important point is that you use no will power or mental coercion in this mental and spiritual exercise."

Sophie went away determined to try the approach I had suggested. A few days later, she called in excitement. That morning she had found herself wide awake an hour before the alarm went off. In her mind, as clear and complete as could be, was an original way to deal with the crucial project. She went to her computer at once. By her usual breakfast hour, she had finished the section of the project that had been giving her trouble for so long.

She Discovered the Riches of Her Creative Thought

A young woman, Marie G., was seriously worried about her mother, who suffered from chronic stomach pains. The mother's doctor had tried a variety of medications, but none of them relieved her distress. An examination of the gastrointestinal system with a fiber-optic probe showed signs of irritation, but did not reveal the *cause* of the irritation. Marie decided that only the healing power of the subconscious mind could help her mother. She began to set aside half an hour every morning and evening to pray for her mother's stomach. She focused on the concept that her mother's digestive system was a Divine idea and therefore perfect.

Unfortunately, Marie's mother's condition did not improve. Still more upsetting, Marie began to have stomach trouble herself.

Marie came to me and begged me to say where she had gone wrong. Why had her prayer caused her subconscious to manifest sickness instead of the desired health?

"By praying as you did," I explained, "you were actually identifying with your mother's illness. You were even keeping a regular date with it, twice a day. What you wanted was to get rid of it, but what you were doing was holding onto it."

How Her Creative Thought Healed

At my suggestion, Marie G. changed her approach. She carefully avoided dwelling on specific organs of the body and their disorders. Instead, she identified with the Infinite Healing Presence in the subconscious mind. She began to claim quietly, feelingly, and lovingly that the Healing Presence and Intelligence in the subconscious, which created her mother's body, was vitalizing, healing, and restoring her whole being into harmony, health, peace, and wholeness. She meditated quietly on these ideas for a short period of time each night before going to sleep. The results were remarkable. Her own stomach distress cleared up immediately, and her mother's problems showed a marked and steady improvement.

Sympathy Versus Compassion

The reason Marie G. became ill while praying for her mother was because she was actually sympathizing with her. We are taught that sympathy is a wonderful quality and that we should all cultivate it. This is an error. Sympathy is like spotting someone trapped in a pool of quicksand and wading in to share their danger. A better reaction, one of *compassion,* would be to stay on firm ground and throw the person a rope or tree branch. When, through sympathy, we accede to the negative or baleful aspects of a person's situation or condition, we tend to aggravate the problem. The reason for this is that the subconscious magnifies exceedingly whatever we focus our attention on.

Giving the Riches of the Infinite to the Sick Person

All the riches of the Infinite, such as inspiration, guidance, faith, abundance, and security, are within you. When you visit people who are sick, lift them up in your thoughts and feelings. Give them a transfusion of faith and confidence in the healing power of the subconscious. Remember that with God all things are possible. Visualize them as whole, radiant, joyous, and free. To feel sorry for the ill person and to commiserate with him or her is to drag the person down. This is a negative approach. Be compassionate and call forth the infinite healing presence in the subconscious, which can heal, bless, and restore both mind and body. *He restoreth my soul* (Psalm 23:3).

You Are the Master of Your Thoughts— Not the Servant

Your thought is creative. Every thought tends to manifest itself and causes your subconscious mind to respond according to the nature of the thought. You can direct and steer your thoughts just as you steer your car. Thoughts are things—material changes in the pattern of the universe. Your thought-image is a reality in your mind and the basis for what we call external reality. A car is a solid, material object, but if every car in the world suddenly vanished, an automotive engineer could quickly redesign the vehicle based on the thought-image in his or her mind. In a short while, we could again have millions of cars.

Your thought is the most powerful instrument you have to work with, infinitely more powerful than the latest computer. It pays fabulous dividends to learn to direct your thoughts wisely, constructively, and judiciously. Your thought works with mathematical exactitude: It creates limitation and lack if you dwell on ideas of poverty, and it brings expansion, growth, and prosperity when you think along these lines.

Become a Good Executive

It takes a good executive to draw forth the riches of the subconscious mind. You can tell good executives by the way they handle tasks. They have the mental acumen and sagacity to pick the best person for the task and delegate it to him or her. Once they have passed the task along, they keep their hands off and give the other person enough space to get on with it. Poor executives, on the other hand, whether in business, science, art, industry, or education, are constantly meddling with the pie they have asked others to bake.

When you pray, you must be a good executive. Learn to delegate authority to your subconscious mind. It knows all and sees all. It will bring your prayer to pass in its own way. When you pray or seek an answer, turn your request or desire over to your subconscious mind with complete faith and confidence, knowing that whatever is conveyed to the subconscious will come to pass.

How do you know if you have really turned your request over with faith and confidence? By the way you feel. If you constantly wonder how, when, where, and through what source your prayer will be answered, if you are anxious and apprehensive, you do not really trust the wisdom of your subconscious. Stop nagging your subconscious. The negativity of your worries will tend to bring forth fruit after its kind. When you think of your desire, lightness of touch is important. Remind yourself that Infinite Intelligence is taking care of it in Divine order.

Her Thought Is the Magnet

Lisa M. is a very successful stockbroker. She told me that she owes all her success to the fact that she maintains a mental picture of success in her work. This acts as a sort of magnet that attracts to her the clients and conditions that accurately correspond to her thoughts and feelings.

This is her prayer every morning: "I am a mental and spiritual magnet. I draw to me all those people who want and need what I have to offer. There is a Divine exchange of ideas between us; they are blessed and I am blessed. I decree harmony, abundance, right action, and inspiration, and I know my subconscious mind accepts these truths."

Lisa finds herself Divinely led and directed in all she does. Her subconscious mind is the seat of habit. As she continues to claim Divine guidance, right action, and abundance regularly and systematically, she is under a subconscious compulsion to do, speak, and act in the right way.

How He Conquered by Surrendering

I recently had a long conversation with a prominent banker, Brendan O. A friend had told him that I might be able to help him give up tobacco. Though skeptical, he was desperate enough to try anything. As we talked, I began to see that he was involved in waging a daily war with the world and its conditions. He saw every associate as a possible rival and pored over their every word for hints of what hostile, underhanded act to expect from them. As he read the business section of the paper each morning, he muttered curses. Each new development felt like a blow aimed directly at him. It is no wonder that he was a heavy smoker. Eventually, his doctor told him he had to quit. He pooh-poohed the idea. Then one day, breathlessness forced him to quit his weekly tennis game . . . while he was ahead. That was enough to make him decide to stop.

Of course, he approached the task of quitting smoking the same way he approached everything else—as a battle. It didn't work. The harder he tried to quit, the more restless and irritable he became, and the more he felt the urge to smoke. His nerves were shot. He began to make risky business decisions and to act toward his superiors as badly as he did to those under him. Soon his entire career was in serious danger. By the time we spoke, he was beginning to consider the idea of ending it all.

"You are like someone who has strayed into a patch of quicksand," I told him. "The harder you struggle, the deeper you sink. Not just with the smoking, though that is very important. The war you think you are waging against the world, you are really waging against your own subconscious mind. Every day you tell it that life is full of conflict and hostility, and every day it takes you at your word and makes manifest the conditions you expect."

"But I really *want* to stop smoking," Brendan protested.

"I don't doubt it," I replied. "But you are overlooking a basic law of mind. When your desire and imagination are in conflict, your imagination always wins. You imagine yourself struggling against tobacco, and you provoke that very struggle."

"Maybe so," he said. "But now I'm in the thick of it, and I can't afford to lose. We're talking about my life and health that are at stake. What do I have to do to win this battle?"

I took a deep breath. This was not going to be easy. "You have to surrender," I told him. "Give up. Abandon the struggle."

"Never!" he broke in. "Roll over and play dead? Never!"

"I didn't say play dead," I said calmly. "What you must do is find the path to invoking a greater power. And the entrance to that path lies in the opposite direction from struggle."

Suddenly his shoulders slumped. "I don't get it," he said in a low voice. "But I'm ready to try anything. What do I do now?"

He Found the Quiet Path to Get Things Done

At my suggestion, Brendan held a session with himself twice a day, on first getting up and just before going to sleep. He sat in a quiet place and breathed calmly and steadily, until he felt himself become relaxed and receptive. Then he affirmed and visualized as follows:

> Freedom and peace of mind are mine now. I know that as I believe and affirm these truths, they are sinking down into my subconscious mind. I will be under compulsion to give up cigarettes, as the law of my subconscious is compulsion. In my

imagination I see my doctor before me. He has just finished examining me and is congratulating me on my freedom from the habit and on my perfect health.

As these sessions continued, he got a response from his subconscious. His desire to smoke faded until it was gone. He had succeeded in impregnating his deeper mind with his habitual thinking and visualizing. The next time he saw his doctor, he learned that the worrisome symptoms had faded as well. He was in excellent health.

Brendan's new approach to his subconscious mind had more widespread effects, too. He found himself calmer and more collegial at work, and his business judgment improved. He realizes now that it is the quiet mind that gets things done. Though it is months since he last felt the desire to smoke, he continues to hold sessions with himself twice a day. He quiets his body and tells it to be still and relaxed. It has to obey. When his conscious mind is quiet, calm, peaceful, and receptive, the wisdom of his subconscious rises to the surface, and he receives marvelous answers and solutions.

The Riches of Letting Go and Letting God Help

A psychologist named Sylvia B. got dragged into a bitter and complex legal case involving a former patient. The many documents and frequent court appearances became a terrible drain on her time and energy. When she tried to be conscientious about her participation, she found that she had no room left for living her own life. At last she realized that she was neglecting the greatest power she had available to her. She turned to her subconscious and prayed as follows:

> Divine wisdom and Divine right action of my subconscious, solve this problem. I release the matter and let it go.

Whenever she had to get in touch with her attorney or others involved in the case, she would silently decree:

> The God-Presence within me is all-wise and is taking care of this in Divine order. I am not keeping tabs on the God-Presence within as to how, when, where, or through what source this will be solved. I let go and let God take care of it.

The sequel to her new attitude of mind was interesting. Her former patient admitted fault and begged her forgiveness. The suit was dismissed immediately. There was a Divine adjustment, and she was set free from all legal entanglements.

The Future Can Be Wonderful for You

Do not waste your energy and vital substance by brooding over old peeves, grudges, and grievances. To do so is like ripping open a grave—all you find is a skeleton. Focus your attention on the good things of life. Realize that the future will be wonderful because your harmonious thoughts will germinate and grow, bringing forth wonderful fruit: health, happiness, abundance, and peace of mind.

Draw a thick line under the past, then turn the page. Never mentally touch any negative experience or trauma that has happened in the past. Remain faithful to this mental attitude and realize that as you change your present thoughts and keep them changed, you will change your destiny.

She Discovered the Riches of Scientific Prayer

Anna H. came to me distraught and highly agitated. Her 18-year-old son had left home following an argument with his father. He dropped out of college and wrote that he was planning to join a cult. Anna was so frantic that her doctor put her on powerful tranquilizers and antidepressants. She was also resorting to sleeping pills almost every night.

During our conversation, I tried to point out a few simple truths. "You do not own your son," I told her. "Yes, he came *through* you, but not *by* you. The Life-Principle is our common progenitor. We are all children of the one Father, or Self-Originating Spirit. Your son is here to grow, to expand, and to overcome difficulties, challenges, and problems. He must discover for himself the powers within him. It is up to him to release his talents to the world. You can't help him by mental excitation, anger, and resentment, only through love, understanding, and right action."

By the end of our conversation, Anna had decided to release her son completely. Sincerely, feelingly, and with deep confidence, she decreed as follows:

> I loose my son to God completely. He is Divinely guided in all his ways and Divine wisdom anoints his intellect. Divine law and order reign supreme in his life. He is guided to his true place and is expressing himself at his highest level. I loose him and let him go.

She remained faithful to this prayer. Twice every day she claimed peace, harmony, joy, and Divine love for her son and for herself. Some weeks later, she got a phone call from her son. He had become disillusioned with his new "associates." He realized that their only goal was to mold his thoughts to fit their own. They had no intention to let him find and be himself. He was returning to college with the goal of learning more about the spiritual wisdom of the ages.

Since then, Anna's son has done well in his scholastic work. He has also started meditating daily and writing some of the thoughts that come to him in meditation. He communicates frequently with both his parents, but his mother no longer feels possessive. She has discovered the riches of Divine love and freedom.

When Anna stopped thinking from the standpoint of circumstances and conditions, she began to discover that interior standpoint where there are no circumstances. From there, she was able to decree what conditions should be according to Divine law and order. Then she let the wisdom of her subconscious take care of it.

How to Think Richly

Think regularly and systematically of life, illumination, inspirations, harmony, prosperity, happiness, peace, and the life more abundant. Think these truths rather than this or that condition on them. Trust the operations of your subconscious mind to bring all these ideas you are contemplating into being in the way best suited for your particular case. This is a wonderful way to enter into the life more abundant.

MEDITATION TO HAVE THE POWER OF FAITH

Use the following meditation to help you secure the power of faith:

> *"The prayer of faith shall save the sick and God shall raise him up."* (James 5:15) I know that no matter what the negation of yesterday was, my prayer or affirmation of truth will rise triumphantly over it today. I steadfastly behold the joy of the answered prayer. I walk all day long in the Light.
>
> Today is God's day; it is a glorious day for me, as it is full of peace, harmony, and joy. My faith in the good is written in my heart and felt in my inward parts. I am absolutely convinced that there is a Presence and a perfect Law that receives the impress of my desire now and that irresistibly attracts into my experience all the good things my heart desires. I now place all my reliance, faith, and trust in the Power and Presence of God within me; I am at peace.
>
> I know I am a guest of the Infinite and that God is my host. I hear the invitation of the Holy One saying, *"Come unto me*

all ye that labor, and I will give you rest." (Matthew 11:28) I rest in God; all is well.

⌒ CHAPTER POINTS TO REMEMBER ⌒

1. To believe is to accept something as true. Belief makes the difference between success and failure, riches and poverty, health and sickness. Believe in the riches of the Infinite Power within your subconscious and you will experience them.

2. When your problems seem overwhelming, break the tension by praying sincerely for someone who is very ill or in deep trouble, and suddenly you will find your own problems solved.

3. When praying for a loved one, be sure not to identify with the ailment or any part of the anatomy. Realize that the Infinite Healing Presence is flowing through the loved one as harmony, health, peace, and joy. Visualize the loved one as radiant and happy. Meditate quietly on these truths and pray again when you feel led to do so. Wonders happen as you pray this way.

4. Sympathy means to go down into the quicksand with the other, and it does not help the sick person. Have compassion and give the sick person a transfusion of faith, confidence, and love, knowing that with God all things are possible.

5. Your thought is creative, and every thought tends to manifest itself. You can direct and steer your thoughts in the same way you steer your car. Thoughts are things. Your thought-image of wealth, success, and achievement is the magnet that attracts to you all things that correspond with your thought-image.

6. The quiet mind gets things done. Tell your body to be still, and quiet your mind by thinking of the infinite intelligence of your subconscious, which knows the answer.

When your conscious mind is still and your body is re-laxed, the wisdom of your subconscious will rise to the surface mind.

7. A good executive knows how to delegate authority. You must be a good executive when using your mind. Turn your request over to your subconscious with faith and confidence, and you will get the appropriate response. You know when you have really turned it over, because you find yourself at peace.

8. You can give up smoking or any bad habit by decreeing freedom and peace of mind, while at the same time imagining a friend or a physician congratulating you on your freedom. As you affirm and envision an antipathy toward tobacco, your subconscious will take over and compel your freedom from the habit.

9. Many have discovered the wisdom of turning an acute domestic problem over to the God-Presence, trusting that Divine wisdom and intelligence will bring about the solution that is best for all. The prayer, "I let go and let God take over," brings about the perfect answer.

10. Liquidate the past and never dwell on old grievances or grudges. The future is your present thinking made manifest. Think regularly and systematically of harmony, beauty, love, peace, and abundance, and you will have a wonderful future.

11. We do not own our children. When difficulties arise with a child, pray as follows: "I loose my child to God completely. My child is Divinely guided in all ways, and Divine love takes care of my child." Whenever you think of your child, bless him or her silently by knowing, "God loves my child and cares for my child." As you do this, whatever happens will be good.

12. Think of the infinite riches within your subconscious mind. Think of harmony, peace, joy, love, guidance, right action, success—all these are principles of life, and as you think of the life more abundant, you activate the latent powers within you. Your subconscious will compel you to express the abundant life right here and right now. Thoughts are things.

13. Use the meditation to secure the great power of faith for yourself.

3

How the Rich Get Richer—and How You Will Join Them

The Bible says: *God, who giveth us richly all things to enjoy* (I Timothy 6:17). Riches are of your mind. There is a guiding principle within you that can lead you to fulfill the desires of your heart. Wealth is a state of consciousness, a mental attitude, an acceptance of the riches of the Infinite. The whole world was here when you were born. Life was a gift to you. You are here to express life and to release your hidden talents to the world.

Once you gain the ability to tap your subconscious mind, you will never want for any good thing all your life, whether it be health, peace of mind, true expression, companionship, or a lovely home and all the money you need to do what you want to do when you want to do it. Your subconscious offers you the infinite power to be rich, and the key is your own thought. Your thought is creative. Begin to think regularly and systematically of success, achievement, victory, abundance, and the good life. Thinking makes it so.

She Discovered Her Thought-Image Was Wealth

A few years ago I joined a guided tour that took me to many scenic places in Spain and Portugal. There were about 30 of us on this tour. One was a young woman named Maria B. When I introduced myself, during a get-acquainted party at our first stop, her eyes widened.

"Are you the man who wrote *The Power of Your Subconscious Mind*?*" she asked excitedly. "I owe this trip to you!"

She explained that she had always wanted to visit Spain. Her ancestors had originally come from Malaga, one of the places we were scheduled to visit. The expenses of such a tour were beyond her means, however. For a long time, she put the project out of her mind as impossible. When she read about the wonderful powers of her subconscious, however, she decided to put the techniques to the test.

Her first step was to gather brochures and magazine articles about Spain. Looking through them, she found herself mysteriously drawn to a photograph in one of the tourist brochures of the Hotel Malaga Palacio. She decided that this attraction must be a sign from her subconscious. Every night before going to sleep, she would concentrate on the picture. Then she would place herself in a dreamy, receptive state of mind and imagine she was in that hotel. She visualized her room, the beautiful view from her window, the wonderful meals on the terrace, all in as much detail as possible.

After she had followed this procedure for about a week, she happened to take the folder for one of the guided tours to work with her. As she was glancing through it before leaving for lunch, one of her coworkers, a young man whom she didn't know, saw it and remarked how much he wanted to see Spain. They went out to lunch together and discovered they

---

**The Power of Your Subconscious Mind* by Joseph Murphy, revised and expanded by Ian McMahan. Paramus, NJ: Reward Books, 2000.

had a great deal in common. Soon they were dating seriously. When they became engaged, Maria's aunt told her that as a wedding present she wanted to pay for the couple's honeymoon and suggested a tour of Spain.

"So you see," Maria concluded. "I don't just owe you this chance to see Spain. I owe you my marriage, too!"

I smiled. "You don't owe me a thing," I said. "All this you owe to the power of your own subconscious and to your wisdom in making use of it"

Maria's story illustrates the working of your deeper mind. It always magnifies what you deposit in it. She visualized a trip to Malaga. She received not only that, but a new and fulfilling relationship. Your subconscious gives you compound interest. Whatever you deposit in it is magnified and multiplied exceedingly. Maria's thought-image proved to her where all the riches are.

How He Invoked the Law of Increase

On the tour of Spain I just mentioned, we visited the city of Seville, which personifies the real Spain more than any other community in that country. Over half a million people here share a rich history that has included Phoenicians, Romans, Visigoths, and Moors, all of whom left their mark there. Seville's university was founded in 1502, and the city gave the world two of its greatest painters, Murillo and Velasquez.

One of our guides was a friendly, intelligent young man who had a thorough knowledge of the city and its culture, along with a fund of interesting and amusing sidelights. As we were walking from our hotel to the cathedral, I said to him, "Where did you learn your English? You speak like a native."

He grinned. "That's because I am," he said. "I grew up in New York City, in Queens."

"Okay, then I'll rephrase my question," I said. "Where did you learn your Spanish? You speak like a native."

"That's an interesting story," he replied. "My mom is Spanish, from right here in Seville. She and my dad met when he was stationed here with the Air Force. She always talked Spanish to me at home, and of course New York has a lot of Spanish speakers, so I had plenty of chances to practice."

"I can see that," I said. "But what brought you here?"

"For as long as I can remember, I wanted to live in Europe and be a guide," he told me. "I used to read guidebooks the way other kids read mysteries. I loved to study maps. When I daydreamed, I'd daydream about walking through one of the great cities and looking at all the historic buildings. When I was 14, I decided I had to do something to make my dream become real. So I wrote it down on a piece of paper. I said I wanted to learn French and German so I could guide people from many countries around Spain and the rest of Europe. I carried the paper folded in my wallet, and every time I had some spare moments, I took it out and reread it. I told myself it wasn't a dream, it was a reality that simply hadn't happened yet."

I was terrifically impressed by this young man's account. Without conscious knowledge of how the subconscious mind works, he had stumbled upon an effective way of invoking it.

"Well, the fact that you're here, taking us around, proves that you were right," I remarked. "How did the fulfillment of your dream come about?"

"Simple," he replied, with another infectious grin. "So simple I never would have thought of it on my own. My mother's relatives wrote and asked if I'd like to come live with them while I went to high school in Seville. I jumped at it, of course. And when I got here, I learned that the university has a course of study for people who want to go into the tourist industry. So here I am."

This guide's constant prayer is: *The God of Heaven, He will prosper us* (Nehemiah 2:20). By constantly dwelling on his written request, he succeeded in writing it in the tablets of his subconscious mind, which responded by bringing it to pass in its own unique way.

How to Follow Your State of Mind

The Lord maketh poor and maketh rich: he bringeth low and lifteth up (I Samuel 2:7). The Lord is the lordly power of your subconscious mind, called the Father within. Your Lord is what dominates your thinking. If your dominant conviction is that you are entitled to all the good things of life, such as health, wealth, love, true expression, and the abundant life, you will experience accordingly. On the other hand, if you feel that you are destined to be poor and that the good things of life are not for you, you are placing yourself in want, lack, frustration, and self-imposed bondage.

Remember, your thought has power; it is creative. Every thought you initiate tends to manifest itself except if it is neutralized by a more powerful thought of greater intensity. All the men and women who garner more of the world's goods reveal a wealth consciousness and a joyous expectancy of the best. Everything you experience is due to the law of your mind. By dwelling on the idea of increased good and by nourishing it and sustaining it, a person draws more of the riches of life to himself. On the other hand, one who thinks only of decrease, lack, and limitation magnifies his or her loss. The law of your subconscious is to increase any idea implanted in it. The experience of the negative thinker will attract more and more loss.

Begin to Practice the Law of Increase

Remember, any object to which you give special attention will tend to grow and magnify itself in your life. Attention is the key to life. Think of increase along all lines. Feel you are successful and prosperous, and you will see that the feeling of wealth produces wealth. Be sure you wish for all those around you success, happiness, and abundance, knowing that as you wish increase of wealth and happiness for others, you are also attracting more of God's riches to yourself. As you radiate abundance and riches to others, they will pick up your thoughts subconsciously and will be benefitted by the feeling of riches and abundance emanating from you.

You can silently give to all people you meet the following blessing: "God gave you richly all things to enjoy, and you are prospered beyond your fondest dreams." That simple prayer will work wonders in your life.

How to Use the Law of Increase in Your Business or Profession

As you quietly, lovingly, and feelingly enter into the realization that your thoughts of richness, success, prosperity, and health create all those conditions and circumstances on which you focus your attention, you will automatically create all the conditions necessary for your advancement. Moreover, you will find yourself attracting more and more people who will become clients, customers, friends, and associates and who will aid you in the realization of your dreams. You will subconsciously attract to yourself the men and women who are living in the consciousness of God's riches.

I was browsing through an exclusive shop in the Rodeo Drive section of Beverly Hills when a fashionably dressed woman came over to me. She introduced herself as Rhonda M., the founder and owner of the shop. As we talked, she told me what she regards as the secret of her tremendous success and great popularity with her customers. Every morning as she opens the store, she decrees: "Everyone who enters here is blessed and prospered, inspired and enriched in all ways." She has learned a great truth, which is: *Thou shalt also decree a thing, and it shall be established unto thee; and the light shall shine upon thy ways* (Job 22:28).

How He Lost His Home

A friend introduced me to Barbara S., who lived with her husband in an upcoming area not far from my home. She confided that she was terribly worried about her husband. An insurance broker, he was constantly dwelling on his financial problems and setbacks.

"I know his business isn't doing well," Barbara told me. "There's so much new competition from Internet-based companies. But it can't be good for him to spend so much time imagining that he'll go bankrupt and that we'll lose our home."

I was alarmed by the picture she painted. "You must try to persuade him to focus on more positive thoughts," I urged her.

"I've tried," she said. "He refuses to listen. It's almost as if he *wants* to fail, so he can say, 'I told you so.'"

A month or so later, my friend told me that Barbara's husband's firm had filed for bankruptcy, and their home was for sale at under its market value. It was snapped up by a wealthy neighbor as an investment.

There are good, solid reasons why the rich get richer and the poor get poorer. Job said: *The thing which I greatly feared is come upon me* (Job 3:25). The law of mind is good and very good. A person who thinks constantly of loss, lack, failure, and bankruptcy cannot expect to prosper and succeed. The rich person walking in the consciousness of success and prosperity looks upon wealth as like the air he breathes. It is his attitude, not merely his wealth, that lets him acquire the former home of the poor person. You can't think evil and reap good, any more than you can think good and reap evil. The law of your mind is perfect. It tries to manifest what is impressed upon it. The poor person, by which I mean the person who doesn't know how to operate and release the riches of her mind, creates her own poverty. She can, however, at any time she wishes, begin to practice the law of opulence and again attract to herself wealth, success, and riches of all kinds.

The Rewards of Being Acquainted with the Law of Opulence

You can get acquainted with the qualities of an orange by tasting it and eating it. You can get acquainted with the riches of your subconscious by applying the law of opulence. A businessman said to me that the source of supply was within him, and he responded to his faith in the endless resources of the infinite riches of his subconscious mind. Every morning and every night his prayer is: "I am ever grateful for God's riches that are ever active, ever present, unchanging and abundant." This businessman never wants for all the money he needs to operate his enterprise and to open up new branches.

Listen to the Truth and You Will Never Be in Want

Infinite Spirit, the source of all blessings, the creator of the world and all things therein contained is within you. You do not own anything in the universe; God, or Spirit, owns all. You are a steward of the Divine and you are here to use the wealth of the world wisely, judiciously, and constructively, claiming Divine wisdom in your handling of all your earthly possessions. When you go on to another dimension, you cannot take with you anything but the treasures of wisdom, truth, and beauty that you have instilled in your subconscious mind. Your faith, confidence, and trust in the goodness of God and in the joy of the Lord that is your strength represent the real riches you will take with you into the next stage of life—these are the treasures of heaven (your mind).

The whole world is yours to enjoy. The cattle on a thousand hills are yours. The songs of the birds are yours. You can enjoy the stars in the heavens, the morning dew, the dusk and the dawn. You can turn your eyes to the hills, the mountains, and the valleys. You can smell the sweet fragrance of the rose and the tang of new-mown hay. All the riches in the soil, in the air, and in the sea are yours. The fruit that falls to the ground and rots is abundant enough to feed all of humanity. Nature is bountiful, lavish, extravagant, even wasteful.

It is God's intention and will that you lead a full and happy life. You should live in a beautiful home, surrounded by luxury. You should have beautiful clothes, constantly dressing for God and reminding yourself of the infinite and indescribable beauty, order, symmetry, and proportion of the Infinite. You should have all the money you need to do what you want to do, when you want to do it. Your children should be brought up in beautiful surroundings and in a loving, Godlike atmosphere. They should be taught the endless resources within the depths of their own minds, so that, being able to tap the riches of their subconscious, they, too, will never want for any good thing.

How to Tap the Endless Source of Supply

Recognize the infinite source within your subconscious, then invoke the great law of opulence and increase as follows:

> God is the source of my supply, whether it is energy, vitality, creative ideas, inspiration, love, peace, beauty, right action, or wealth that I need. I know the creative powers of my subconscious can bring all these things into being. I am now appropriating mentally and experiencing buoyant health, harmony, beauty, right action, abundant prosperity, and all the riches of my deeper mind. I exude vibrancy and goodwill to all. I am giving better service every day. God's riches are forever flowing into my experience, and there is always a Divine surplus. All these thoughts are sinking down into my subconscious, and they are now coming forth as abundance, security, and peace of mind. It is wonderful.

As you sow in your subconscious, so shall you reap. The Bible says: *The wilderness and the solitary place shall be glad for them; and the desert shall rejoice, and blossom as the rose* (Isaiah 35:1).

DAILY MEDITATION FOR THE RICH LIFE

If you repeat the following meditation daily, it will bring the rich life to you faster and easier:

> *Consider the lilies of the field; they toil not, neither do they spin; yet Solomon in all of his glory was not arrayed as one of these.* (Matthew 6:28) I know that God is prospering me in all ways. I am now leading the abundant life, because I believe in a God of abundance. I am supplied with everything that contributes to my beauty, well-being, progress, and peace. I am daily experiencing the fruits of the spirit of God within me; I accept my good now; I walk in the light that all good is mine. I am peaceful, poised, serene, and calm. I am one with the source of life; all my needs are met at every moment of time and every point of space. I now bring "all the empty vessels" to the Father within. The fullness of God is made manifest in all the departments of my life. "All that the Father hath is mine." I rejoice that this is so.

☞ CHAPTER POINTS TO REMEMBER ☜

1. The rich get richer for the simple reason that the consciousness or awareness of wealth and the expectancy of more and more of God's riches, which are omnipresent, attract more and more wealth, health, and opportunities to the person who walks in that state of mind.

2. The thought-image of wealth produces wealth; the thought-image of a journey results in the opportunity to take it. A young woman began to visualize the experience of staying in a hotel in Spain. Her subconscious opened the way and magnified her impression of the journey into a honeymoon. Your subconscious always magnifies.

3. A young boy of 14 wrote down his dream of moving to Europe and studying to be a guide. He continued to meditate on what he had written and succeeded in writing his requests on the book of life (his subconscious) within him. His subconscious wisdom acted on the mind of his relatives, fulfilling all his desires.

4. Enter into a consciousness of God's wealth, which is all around you. Live in the joyous expectancy of the best, and by the law of attraction, you will attract the riches of the Infinite storehouse in your own subconscious mind. Keep thinking of prosperity, abundance, security, and increase in all things.

5. Whatever you give attention to grows, magnifies, and multiplies in your experience. Keep your attention on whatsoever things are lovely and of good report. Radiate abundance, goodwill, and riches to others. They will pick it up subconsciously, and you will attract wonderful people into your life. They will prosper and you will prosper.

6. A rich person walks in the mental attitude that wealth is like the air he or she breathes. Having that state of mind, the person attracts more and more riches of all kinds. The poor person who is constantly picturing and talking of lack, bankruptcy, and hard times attracts these qualities to him or herself.

7. You can get acquainted with the riches of the Infinite storehouse within you by reiterating and believing the following prayer: "I am ever grateful for God's riches that are ever active, ever present, unchanging, and eternal."

8. God gave you richly all things to enjoy in this universe. Life itself is a gift to you. The whole world was here before you were born. Believe and expect the riches of the

Infinite, and invariably the best will come to you. As you practice this simple truth, the desert of your life will rejoice and blossom as the rose.

9. Strengthen your ability to create a rich life by repeating the meditation at the end of the chapter.

How to Claim Your Right to Infinite Riches Now

A few years ago, during the month of May, I took a trip to Ireland, England, and Switzerland. While in Ireland, I went to Killarney to visit a relative of mine. Killarney is one of the world's great beauty spots. For centuries, poets, artists, and writers have struggled to capture the magnificent and varied colors and forms of this wonderland of green mountains and crystal lakes surrounded by luxuriant woods of birch, oak, and arbutus.

It was here amidst the beauty of the countryside that my relative poured out his tale of woe regarding his daughter. Mary (not her real name) was rapidly losing weight. She refused to eat except under pressure from her father. The local doctor had been giving her injections of liver and vitamins, but now said she was a hopeless case. When she was taken to Dublin to see a psychiatrist, she refused to talk to him. Her father was frantic.

I had three long talks with Mary. During the third one, we were sitting on a stone wall with a view of a distant lake when I asked her point-blank: "Mary, are you trying to get even with your father, exerting a sort of revenge, because he prefers your brother to you?"

She stared at me with stricken eyes, then blurted out, "I hate him, I *hate* him! He won't hear a word against Sean, who takes himself off to Dublin and a fine life at the university. It's I stays home and keeps the house, but it's never a kind word I hear, only 'Why did you not do it this way instead?' He'll be a sorry man when I'm gone."

"But, Mary," I said gently, "God intended you to lead a full, happy, and rich life. Your body is a temple of the living God. When you refuse to care for it, that is worse than setting fire to a church."

"I'd never dream of such a thing!" she protested.

"Maybe not, but you're doing it," I replied. "When you refuse to eat, you are destroying your body. There is no difference between that and suicide. Is that really what you want?"

She shook her head. As she turned away, I saw that her eyes had filled with tears.

Her Father Saw His Sad Mistake

I went inside and spoke privately with Mary's father. I told him what she had said. His face turned red, and he began to curse. He shouted that he worked his whole life to support an ungrateful child who had been a bane since the day of her birth.

"Why do you say that?" I asked, when he stopped to take a breath.

He stared at me as if he did not recall who I was or what I was doing there. "She killed my Kate," he said in a flat voice. "I've not had a moment of peace or joy since then. Nor will I until I'm in the churchyard, lying next to Kate once more. May the day come soon!"

I recalled that Kate was the name of his wife, who had died in childbirth. I understood the sad story he had acted out since then, blaming a helpless child for his terrible loss. Now he was in danger of another loss that would be even worse because it was so unnecessary.

"What do you think Kate would say" I asked "if she knew that you hate the child she brought into the world? That that hatred may kill Mary? Would she approve? Would she think that was a proper way to honor her memory?"

For a moment he clenched his fists, as if he thought striking me would relieve his own distress. Then he buried his face in his hands and started to sob. Through his tears, he said, "It's not that I've no tenderness for Mary at all. There are moments when I see her mother in her face, and it breaks my heart. But when I thought of showing it, it was as if I'd be betraying Kate."

"Not betraying," I said. "Glorifying. Honoring her mother in her and the Eternal in Mary, Kate, and all of us."

When I brought Mary in, her father apologized to her and asked forgiveness. He vowed his love, appreciation, and tenderness for her. She was naturally hesitant to believe that he had changed so much, but as he continued to exude and affirm real love for her, he poured forth the riches of the Infinite, and she softened to him.

Mary had been silently saying to herself: "I feel I must starve and die. Nobody loves me. This way I will make my father care for me." Now, with her father's love, she was able to experience her love for herself as well. That evening, I was delighted to see her eat a hearty dinner.

Love frees; it gives; it is the spirit of God. Love opens prison doors and sets free the captives and all those bound by fear, resentment, and hostility.

The Prayer That Changed Her Life

I know my body is the temple where God dwells. I honor and exalt the Divine presence within me. Divine love fills my soul, and His river of peace flows through my mind and heart at all times. I eat my food with joy, knowing that it is transmuted into beauty, harmony, wholeness, and perfection. I know God hath need of me where I am, and I am Divinely expressed. I am loved, I am needed, I am wanted and appreciated by my father and others. I radiate love, peace, and goodwill to everyone at all times. My food and drink are God's ideas that unfold within me, making me strong, wholesome, and full of Divine energy.

Mary is now saturating her subconscious mind with these truths several times a day. In the last letter I received from her she told me she is engaged to marry a neighbor, a young farmer with ambitious ideas. Her words bubbled over with a new life and inner joy. She has truly experienced the riches of the Infinite as love, marriage, inner peace, and abundance.

The Riches of Faith in a Higher Power

After leaving my Irish relatives, I asked my driver to go by way of Glendalough, "The Glen of Two Lakes." Here, in the sixth century, St. Kevin founded a monastery, and his shrine is visited by many people hoping for a cure of various diseases.

My driver told me that as far back as he could remember, he had stuttered badly. In school, the other kids made fun of him and called him "Stutts." Consultations with the finest speech therapists and psychologists in Dublin and Cork City had brought no relief. "Then, when I was eight," he continued, "my da took me to Glendalough He put me in the very cell where St. Kevin stayed and told me, 'Sleep here for an hour, and you'll surely wake healed."

Fascinated, I asked, "And what happened?"

"Sure, I knew my da would never lie to me," he replied. "I did as he said. I went to sleep, there in the cell. And when I woke up, I was healed. Never a bit have I stammered or stuttered from that day to this."

The Real Reason for His Cure

I did not disturb this young man's blind faith, because it was that which had activated and released the healing power of his subconscious mind. This boy's mind at the age of eight was highly impressionable. His imagination was fired by the thought of a miraculous cure. When he was given an unusual ritual to follow, his expectancy was undoubtedly one hundred percent that St. Kevin would intercede for him. It was done unto him as he believed.

There is only one healing power, and that is the Infinite Healing Presence lodged in your subconscious mind.

The Riches of True Faith Versus Blind Faith

True faith consists of knowing that the Infinite Presence that created you from a cell knows all the processes and functions of your body and certainly knows how to heal you. When you consciously tune in on the healing power of your subconscious, knowing and believing it will respond to you, you will get results. In other words, true faith is the combined use of your conscious and subconscious mind scientifically directed for a specific purpose.

Blind faith consists of belief in amulets, charms, talismans, bones of saints, shrines, healing waters, and so on. In other words, it is faith *without* understanding. As a result, its therapeutic value is often only temporary.

I urge people who are sick to seek the help of a physician and to keep on praying not only for themselves but also for the physician.

> *Honour a physician with the honour due unto him for the uses which ye may have of him; for the Lord hath created him.* (Ecclesiasticus, Chapter 38: Paragraphs 1 and 2). For of the Most High cometh healing, and he shall receive honour of the king. . . . The Lord hath created medicines out of the earth; and he that is wise will not abhor them. . . . And he hath given men skill, that he might be honoured in his marvellous works.
>
> My son, in thy sickness be not negligent, but pray unto the Lord, and he will make thee whole . . . Then give place to the

physician, for the Lord hath created him; let him not go from thee, for thou hast need of him. There is a time when in their hands there is good success. For they shall also pray unto the Lord, that he would prosper that which they give for ease and remedy to prolong life . . .

When you pray for health, then health should "spring forth speedily." If it does not, you should take action immediately by going to your medical doctor, dentist, chiropractor, or surgeon, as seems most appropriate to you. Remember, if you were always walking in the consciousness of God's love and peace, you would never be ill, but all of us fall short from time to time. If your teeth are bad and faith does not heal them, I suggest you go immediately to a dentist. Pray that God is guiding him or her and that Divine law and order reign supreme in your life, and you will be satisfied with your new bridgework.

Why He Did Not Experience the Healing Riches of the Infinite

A friend of mine in Waterford, Ireland, Roger C., arranged for me to tour the Waterford glass factory, where the legendary crystal is made. It was an inspiration to watch the skilled craftspeople making the raw glass bloom into depth and sparkle. One of the workers held up the vase he was working on, catching the light on the cut crystal. Then the real glory of its facets, diamonds, flutings, and ovals shone forth in a spectrum of indescribable beauty.

I noticed that Roger was walking with great difficulty, with the help of a cane. I asked him if he was getting proper medical treatment for his condition.

"Oh, yes," he replied. "I have regular cortisone injections, and I take painkillers every day. They help, of course, but not that much. Tell me, for I know you are an expert on these matters. Last year, on a visit to Scotland, I went to a church healing meeting. There was a great crowd there, in a state of great excitement. There were cripples who threw away their crutches, people who said they could hear for the first time, even a woman whose tumor shrank before our eyes."

"And you?" I asked. "How were you affected?"

"That's the odd part," he said. "When the healer touched me, I felt a strong vibration all through my body. For the first time in years, I put down my cane and walked without pain. But the next day I was as lame as ever. Can you explain that?"

He Had a Temporary Emotional Healing

"I think I can," I told Roger. "The press of the crowd, the glare of the lights, the music and chanting and emotional atmosphere combined to put you in a very susceptible state. When the so-called 'healer' placed his hands on you, he probably manipulated your leg, called on Jesus to heal you, then told you to rise up and walk."

Roger gave me an astonished look. "That's exactly the way it was!"

"In the sensitive state you were in," I continued, "your subconscious mind summoned up the power to let you walk temporarily without your cane. At the same time, you took in a hypnotic suggestion that blocked the experience of pain for a day. However, hypnotic suggestions to the subconscious soon wear off. And that is what happened to you."

On the Road to Recovery

Roger began to see that he had not reached the cause of his condition. He began to understand that true, permanent healing comes with forgiveness, love, goodwill to all, and spiritual insight—all these are real healing forces. He admitted he was seething with hostility, guilt, resentment, and hatred toward many people, especially those who were not crippled as he was. He began to realize that his destructive emotions contributed to his condition. I suggested that he cooperate with his doctor and pray for him and also bless him, which he promised to do.

The Prayer That Is Helping My Arthritic Friend

At Roger's request, I wrote out a prayer for him.

> I forgive myself for harboring negative, destructive thoughts about myself and others. I fully and freely forgive everyone, and I sincerely wish for them health, happiness, and all the blessings of life. Whenever a person comes into my mind whom I dislike, I will immediately affirm, "I have released you. God be with you." I know when I have forgiven others, because I feel no sting in my mind. The Infinite Healing Presence of God flows through me, and His river of peace flows through me. I know that Divine love saturates my entire being, and God's love dissolves everything unlike itself. The Healing Light of God is focused at that point in my mind where the problem is, and it is shattered, making way for the Holy Spirit (spirit of wholeness) to indwell every thought and every cell. I give thanks for the healing that is taking place now, for I know all healing is of the Most High. I know God is guiding my doctor, and whatever He does will bless me.

He has been reiterating these truths slowly, quietly, and feelingly morning and night, knowing all the while that these spiritual vibrations will enter into his subconscious mind, obliterating the negative patterns lodged there by years of vicious and destructive thinking. The second letter I received from him said that his physician is amazed at his progress and is planning to refer him to a physical therapist for retraining in walking without a cane. He is well on the road to a real spiritual healing, for all healing is of the Most High. *I am the Lord that healeth thee* (Exodus 15:26).

How the Riches of Belief Pay Dividends in All Phases of Life

Five miles from Cork City is the celebrated landmark Blarney Castle. Its greatest source of fame is the "Blarney Stone," which is set high into the outer wall. According to legend, those who kiss the Blarney Stone become blessed with the "gift of gab." Because of this legend, the word "blarney," has come to mean pleasing talk, intended to deceive without offending. People come from around the globe to kiss the Blarney Stone. This is not an easy matter. You have to lie on your back, grasp an iron railing, and lean out backwards over a daunting fall. But afterwards, you are supposed to develop marvelous powers of speech.

While visiting the castle, I fell into conversation with Father B., an Irish priest. When I brought up the legend of the Blarney Stone, he said, "You mustn't scoff. I've had proof of its powers myself."

"Oh?" I said. "How's that?"

"When I entered the priesthood, I was a terrible bore," he confessed. "When I was scheduled to give the sermon, the church would be almost empty. I even began to question my vocation. Then on a visit here, I kissed the Stone, just for the doing of it. But afterwards, my sermons improved. There are now those kind enough to call me an orator. Be that as it may, when I preach, many come to listen. It is just as the Gospel says: *All things are possible to him that believeth* (Mark 9:23)."

Any geologist will tell you that a block of stone is simply a block of stone, even if it is part of the wall of a famous castle. It has no power to confer the gift of oratory or eloquence. Even so, kissing it may well have that effect, as it did with Father B. How? Because our beliefs and expectancies stir up the dormant powers in the depths of the subconscious mind. Those powers were always there, waiting to be recognized and utilized. *Wherefore, I put thee in remembrance that thou stir up the gift of God, which is in thee* (II Timothy 1:6).

The Instant Riches of Mental Insight and Understanding

At another point in my visit to Ireland, I went on a pony trek to the Gap of Dunloe in Killarney. Riding through this gap on a sturdy Kerry pony was a memorable thrill. During the last

Ice Age, glaciers carved a path through the surrounding hills. The towering summits of the Reeks, the changing shadows on the mountain tops, and the silence and solitude of the cliff-bound road combined to make an unforgettable impression on me.

One of my companions on the ride was a young Englishman, Basil F. As we reached the middle stretch of the narrow gorge, he suffered an acute asthma attack. Fortunately, he was well prepared, with a prescription inhaler as well as a hypodermic kit of adrenaline in case the attack became really severe.

After the attack subsided, he confided that he had to deal with this practically every day, almost always around noon.

"It's no wonder I have asthma," he added. "My father had it all his life. I was there when he died from an attack. It was terrible."

Puzzled, I asked, "Didn't you mention earlier that you were an adopted child?"

"Yes, that's right," he agreed. "I was adopted as a baby."

He did not seem to notice the contradiction in his thinking. He attributed his asthma to heredity, while at the same time telling me he was adopted. That, of course, ruled out any hereditary source of his illness.

How His Mental and Emotional Disturbance Released

Later, during a break, Basil and I went aside and had a deeply personal talk. I confronted him with the contradiction I had remarked on earlier. At first he argued, but then he admitted that he had hated his adopted father.

"Why was that?" I asked sympathetically. "Did something happen to make you feel that way?"

"Oh, yes, indeed," he replied. "I must have been twelve at the time. I did something to make him angry, something quite trivial really. He told me, 'You are no son of mine. You're someone's castoff bastard. I took you out of the gutter and gave you a home, and this is how you repay my kindness!'"

I was shocked. "And that was the first time you learned you were adopted?"

"Just so." His eyes glistened with tears. "I hated him for that. But he was right. I was repaying his kindness with anger and resentment. I was acting exactly like what he had called me."

"Do you think it was kind of him to tell you something so important in a moment of anger?" I asked.

"No, I suppose not," he said slowly. "But I must have been a terrible trial, or he would not have done it."

During his adolescent years, Basil tried to deny his anger and resentment toward his adopted father, but it remained suppressed in the deeper recesses of his mind. Being a negative and destructive emotion, it had to have an outlet sooner or later. When his adopted father died, he took on the older man's symptoms of asthma as a form of self-punishment for his sins.

I explained this to him fully. I then pointed out that though he undoubtedly deeply resented the fact that he was born out of wedlock, there is no such thing as an illegitimate child in the eyes of God. The real illegitimate child is one who thinks negatively and fails to conform to the Golden Rule and the Law of Love. He had developed the symptom because he felt he should suffer for his sense of unworthiness and self-rejection, plus his hatred and antagonism for the man who had adopted him. I pointed out that his adopted father had tried to do the best he could for him. He should work toward forgiving him for that angry, hurtful outburst.

Basil understood immediately. On the rest of the ride, he was quiet and thoughtful. When we returned to our hotel in Killarney, I gave him a copy of *The Power of Your Subconscious Mind* * and wrote out a special prayer for him to use

---

The Power of Your Subconscious Mind by Joseph Murphy, revised and expanded by Ian McMahan. Paramus, NJ: Reward Books, 2000.

regularly every day. I also urged him to continue cooperating with his physician.

This is the prayer I gave him:

> I release my foster father and my real father and mother, known only in Divine mind, to God completely. I forgive myself for harboring negative and destructive thoughts about myself and others, and I resolve not to do this anymore. Whenever negative thoughts come to me, I will immediately affirm, "God's love fills my soul." I am relaxed, poised, serene, and calm. God guides my doctor in all his ministrations to me. The breath of the Almighty gave me life, and I know God breathed into me the breath of life and made me a living soul with all the powers and attributes of God within me. I inhale the peace of God and exhale the love of God, and God flows through me as harmony, joy, love, peace, wholeness, and perfection.

I suggested that he affirm these great truths for about five minutes morning, afternoon, and night and that he be careful never to deny what he affirms. When fearful thoughts or approaching symptoms come, he is to say quietly, "I inhale the peace of God and I exhale the love of God to all."

Not long after my return home to California, I received a lovely letter from him. He had been completely free of asthma attacks since our conversation. Truly, the explanation is oftentimes the cure.

The Riches of Forgiveness

In England, I signed up for a tour of Shakespeare country, which still retains much of the flavor that must have influenced the life and work of the immortal poet and playwright. During lunch, at a historic inn in Warwick, I shared a table with a young woman who introduced herself as Margaret R. and mentioned that she was a hospital nurse. When I told her I wrote about the psychological and spiritual dimensions of people's problems, she told me that for the past several months she had suffered a persistent skin rash. She had consulted eminent dermatologists attached to the hospital where she worked, and they had prescribed various lotions and ointments, but all to no avail.

"I'm sure it must be psychosomatic," she added. "But it's no help knowing that, is it now?"

"That depends," I replied. "Experts on psychosomatic illness have said that the skin is where the inner and the outer worlds meet. According to them, many skin conditions are caused by negative emotions such as hostility and resentment. In other words, the skin functions as a sort of organ of elimination. The mental poisons that result from repressed emotions such as guilt, anxiety, and remorse become translated into physical symptoms."

Her face became thoughtful. "That is a very interesting idea," she said. "Will you be in England long? I should very much like to have a consultation with you, if possible."

"Certainly," I said. We picked a date and time, and I gave her the address of the St. Ermin's Hotel, Caxton Street, where I have always stayed when visiting London.

The Cause of Her Itching and Persistent Skin Rash

A few days later, Margaret and I sat in a private alcove of the hotel lobby. I was quite frank with her. I said I sensed she felt very guilty about something and believed she deserved punishment for it. A bottled-up emotion repressed in the subconscious will often express itself in the form of a bodily symptom. If she confessed and cleansed her mind, the itching rash might well disappear.

Looking away in embarrassment, she said, "There *is* something. I am married, but my husband's work has called him abroad. During the last 14 months, I have seen him only once, on holiday."

"Yes?" I prompted. "That must be difficult for you."

"Oh, it is," she replied. "And . . . well, there is one of the doctors at the hospital. He was so sympathetic. We started seeing each other outside of work, and . . . do I have to finish?"

"It would be better if you did," I told her.

"Very well." Her cheeks reddened. "We have entered into a sexual relationship."

She went on to say that she felt filled with remorse and guilt. She was sure that her rash was God's way of punishing her for her sin.

Self-Forgiveness Brings Peace and Release

I explained to Margaret that God, or the Life-Principle, never punishes. People punish themselves by their misuse of the laws of mind. For example, if you cut yourself, the Life-Principle proceeds to call forth a supply of clotting agent, and the subjective intelligence builds a bridge and forms new tissue. If you burn yourself, the Life-Principle holds no grudge, but it seeks to restore your skin to normal by reducing the edema, giving you new skin and tissue. If you take in something harmful, the Life-Principle causes you to regurgitate it. It always seeks to restore you to health. The tendency of the Life-Principle (God) is to heal, restore, and make you whole.

As a nurse, Margaret understood all this at once. Then I asked a pertinent question. "Do you want to be free of this rash?"

Without any hesitation, she said, "Yes, I do."

"Then," I said, "we have no problem. All you have to do is to stop doing what you are now doing and forgive yourself, and that's the end of your trouble."

Before our consultation ended, Margaret had reached a decision to give up the relationship with the doctor and to stop condemning herself.

As I explained to her, self-condemnation and self-criticism are destructive mental poisons that infect the whole system.

They rob you of vitality, vigor, wholeness, and strength and leave you a physical and mental wreck. I pointed out to her that all she had to do was to get her thoughts to conform to the Divine law of harmony and love. A new beginning is a new end.

We prayed together, claiming that Divine love, peace, and harmony were now saturating her entire being and that she was Divinely guided and watched over by an overshadowing Presence. During a long silence, we dwelt on one thing only: The Healing Power of God's love. Then I reminded her of a great truth that should be indelibly imprinted in the minds and hearts of all: *This one thing I do, forgetting those things which are behind, and reaching forth unto those things which are before, I press toward the mark for the prize* (Philippians 3:13, 14).

The prize she sought was health, happiness, and peace of mind. At the end of our meditation, an inner light glowed in her eyes. She told me she had felt something happen to her in the silence. The rash had disappeared completely. We joined together in saying, *Father, I thank thee that thou hast heard me. And I know that thou hearest me always* (John 11:41,42).

The Riches of Wisdom and Understanding

While I was in London, an old friend came to visit me at St. Ermin's Hotel. She brought along her son, Edward, who was 12 at the time. At one point, she confided that Edward was terribly afraid of the dark. This had been going on for two years. I asked her if anything had happened two years earlier that might have given the child a great shock. The subconscious mind never forgets any experience, even if it is blocked from our conscious awareness.

"Why, yes," she said. "We were living in Liverpool at the time, and the house caught fire during the night. My husband had to carry Edward out in his arms, with his coat over him to protect him from the smoke. It was terrible."

"Daddy tried to smother me," Edward suddenly exclaimed. "I couldn't breathe!"

Those two sentences gave us the key to the whole problem. Of course the child was afraid of the dark. In the dark, as he believed, his own father had tried to murder him!

We explained to Edward that in reality his father had been trying to protect him and save his life. We talked about the peril of smoke inhalation, which kills many more people in fires than the flames do, then said that he should radiate love to his father and mother. I counseled the boy and his mother, explaining that no matter what had happened in the past, it could be changed now by filling the subconscious mind with life-giving patterns. There is no time or space in mind, and the lower is always subject to the higher. Filling the boy's mind with the truths of God would crowd out of his mind everything unlike God.

I gave the mother a prayer for her boy. I also asked Edward to use it before sleep. This is the prayer the mother used:

> My boy is God's son. God loves him and cares for him. God's peace fills his soul. He is poised, serene, calm, relaxed, and at ease. The joy of the Lord is his strength. The Healing Presence flows through him as harmony, peace, joy, love, and perfection. God is, and His Presence vitalizes, energizes, and restores his whole being to wholeness, beauty, and perfection. He sleeps in peace and wakes in joy.

For Edward's use she changed the "him" to "me" and had him repeat, "I am God's son," and so on. On my return home, I was delighted to receive a letter from the mother. "My boy is healed," she wrote. "He had a vision in his sleep. A sage appeared in a dream and said to him, 'You are free. Tell your mother.' It was very vivid."

This was the subconscious of the boy revealing to him his healing. *I the Lord will make myself known unto him in a vision, and will speak unto him in a dream* (Numbers 12:6).

A MEDITATION FOR AN EFFECTIVE PROSPERITY PRAYER

Meditate often by repeating the following prayer for prosperity:

Thou shalt make thy way prosperous, and then thou have good success. (Joshua 1:8) I now give a pattern of success and prosperity to the deeper mind within me, which is the law. I now identify myself with the Infinite source of supply. I listen to the still, small voice of God within me. This inner voice leads, guides, and governs all my activities. I am one with the abundance of God. I know and believe that there are new and better ways of conducting my business; Infinite Intelligence reveals the new ways to me.

I am growing in wisdom and understanding. My business is God's business. I am Divinely prospered in all ways. Divine wisdom within me reveals the ways and means by which all my affairs are adjusted in the right way immediately.

The words of faith and conviction that I now speak up open all the necessary doors or avenues for my success and prosperity. I know that *The Lord (Law) will perfect that which concerneth me.* (Psalms 138:8) My feet are kept in the perfect path, because I am a child of the Living God.

⌾ CHAPTER POINTS TO REMEMBER ⌾

1. Resentment and hostility are mental poisons that rob you of vitality, enthusiasm, and energy. A severe eating disorder is often a disguised form of committing suicide, a way of seeking revenge against someone else. The answer is to open the mind and heart to the influx of

Divine love and to realize that others really do care and love you, bringing about a healing and a transformation.

2. When you begin to realize that you are an organ of God and that God hath need of you where you are and that you are loved, needed, and wanted, a complete transformation takes place; you begin to release the riches of the Infinite as love, goodwill, inner peace, and abundance.

3. Often blind faith will bring about remarkable results. Paracelsus said, "Whether the object of your faith be true or false, you will get results." A young boy who stuttered fired his imagination into a joyous expectancy and blind faith and believed that if he slept in the cell where St. Kevin was supposed to have slept, he would be healed. His subconscious accepted his belief, and he was healed.

4. True faith consists of the belief that the Infinite Presence that created you knows all the processes and functions of your body and that when you unite with it believingly, results will follow. True faith is the combined use of your conscious and subconscious mind, scientifically directed.

5. When you pray for health, then health should "spring forth speedily." (Isaiah 58:8) If it does not, go to a doctor immediately and follow the injunction of the Bible, which says: *Honour a physician with the honour due unto him . . . for the Lord hath created him* (Ecclesiasticus, Chapter 38, Paragraph 1).

6. Some people experience excessive emotionalism at public healing meetings; their emotional hysteria often brings a temporary alleviation of pain. These hypnotic suggestions have only temporary effect, however. In true healing, your conscious and subconscious mind must agree, and you must believe in your heart in the Infinite Healing Presence. Then the result is permanent, not temporary. When you pray for healing, complete forgiveness

must take the place of all guilt, peeves, and grudges. You know when you have forgiven others, because there is no sting in your mind.

7. There is no power in sticks, stones, amulets, charms, or bones of saints. But if a person believes that the bone of a dog is that of a saint and that kissing it will bring a healing, it is not the bone of the dog that heals, it is the response of the person's subconscious mind to blind belief.

8. Negative and destructive emotions snarl up in the subconscious mind and cause many diseases. When a person feels guilty, he feels he should be punished, but what he fails to see is that he is punishing himself. When a boy's adopted father died, he took on the dead man's symptoms as a form of self-punishment for his guilt.

9. A wonderful prayer for forgiveness is this: "I forgive myself for harboring negative and destructive thoughts about myself and others, and I resolve not to do this any more. Whenever a negative thought comes to me, I will immediately affirm, 'God's love fills my soul.'"

10. Your skin is where the inner and the outer worlds meet. Emotions of hostility, anger, suppressed rage, and resentment may express themselves as skin diseases. Remorse and guilt, according to psychosomatic physicians, are the cause of many skin eruptions.

11. The Life-Principle (God) never punishes. This Presence always seeks to heal you and to make you whole. Self-condemnation and self-criticism are destructive mental poisons that send psychic pus all over your system, leaving you a physical and mental wreck.

12. Come to a decision. Forget the past and saturate your mind with Divine love, peace, and harmony. Realize that Divine love dissolves everything unlike itself.

13. No matter what has happened in the past, you can change it now. Fill your subconscious with life-giving patterns of thought and you will erase and crowd out everything unlike God.

14. The meditation at the end of the chapter will help you to improve your life and make your way prosperous.

5

How Miracle Thought-Forms Will Increase Your Wealth

The whole world and all its treasures in the sea, air and earth were here before you were born. Begin to think of the untold and undiscovered riches all around you, waiting for the intelligence of humankind to bring them forth. There are more millionaires and billionaires now in the United States than at any previous time in history. A single idea, projected into reality, can bring you a fortune. You are here to release the imprisoned splendor within you and surround yourself with luxury, beauty, and the riches of life. The sooner you begin, the better for you and for the whole world.

Make Friends with Money and You Will Always Have Money

Nothing is so necessary as having the right attitude toward money. Once you make friends with money, you will always have a surplus of it. It is normal and natural for you to desire a fuller, richer, happier, and more wonderful life. Understand that money is God's means of maintaining the economic health of the nations of the world. When money is circulating freely in your life, you are economically healthy. Begin now to see money in its true significance and role in life as a symbol of exchange. Money to you should mean freedom from want; it should mean beauty, luxury, abundance, sense of security, and refinement.

Why She Did Not Have More Money

Being poor is first of all a mental attitude. Judy G. is a very good writer who has had several articles accepted for publication, but she said to me, "I don't write for money."

"What's wrong with money?" I responded. "I understand that money is not your only goal when you write. Perhaps you don't think of it at all at that point. But remember, 'the laborer is worthy of his hire.' What you write inspires, lifts up, and encourages others. Why should you not be rewarded for it? Once you adopt the right attitude, you'll find that financial compensation will automatically come to you freely and copiously."

"I hate the thought of it," she said, with a little shudder. "I do not want the honesty of what I write to be ruined by filthy lucre. To tell you the truth, I wish there were no such thing as money. It really is the root of all evil. It spoils everything. That's why the poor are so much warmer and more human than the rich."

"There is no evil in the universe," I told her. "Good and evil stem from the thoughts and motivations of people. All evil comes from a misinterpretation of life and a misuse of the laws of mind. In other words, the only evil is ignorance, and the only consequence is suffering."

"I don't understand," she said.

"Look at it this way," I explained. "Would you call a bar of copper evil? Or a bar of iron? What about gold?"

"That's different," she said quickly.

"Of course," I agreed. "And what is the difference? A matter of the number and arrangement of the elementary particles.

A $100 bill in itself is nothing more than an innocuous piece of paper. It is our thoughts that give it power and importance, that turn it to good or evil ends."

"I think I see what you mean," she said slowly. "And I'm sure if I had money, I would find ways to do good with it. But I'm afraid of what I'll have to do to get it. Won't that change me and my work? Won't I have to give up my integrity?"

"If that were to happen, it would be another misuse of the laws of mind," I told her. "You are here to develop yourself in all ways. Those include the development and true expression of your talents, as well as the flow of wealth toward you. As for what you have to do, it may be much easier than you think."

She Adopted New Ideas Toward Money and Prospered Accordingly

At my suggestion, Judy adopted a simple technique. The more she practiced it, the more money multiplied in her experience. Every day, before she sat down at her computer to work, she prayed as follows:

> My writings go forth to bless, heal, inspire, elevate, and dignify the minds and hearts of men and women, and I am Divinely compensated in a wonderful way. I look upon money as Divine substance, for everything is made from the One Spirit. I know matter and spirit are one. Money is constantly circulating in my life, and I use it wisely and constructively. Money flows to me freely, joyously, and endlessly. Money is an idea in the mind of God, and it is good and very good.

Judy's changed attitude toward money has worked wonders in her life. She has completely overcome her strange, superstitious beliefs that money is evil and poverty is virtuous. She also realized that it was her subconscious condemnation of money that caused money to fly from her instead of to her. Her income tripled in three months, and that was just the beginning of her financial prosperity.

He Worked Hard but Lacked Money

Some years ago, I talked with a minister, Edwin R., who had a very good following. He had an excellent knowledge of the laws of mind and was able to impart this knowledge to others, but he could never make ends meet. When I asked why he thought that was, he replied by quoting from Timothy: *For the love of money is the root of all evil* (I Timothy 6:10). He neglected what follows later in the same chapter, where the people are charged to place their trust or faith in the living God, *who giveth us richly all things to enjoy* (I Timothy 6:17).

The Bible enjoins us to give our allegiance, loyalty, and faith to the Source of all things, which is God. You are not, therefore, to give your allegiance, loyalty, and trust to created things, but to the Creator, the Eternal Source of everything in the universe. If someone says, "All I want is money, nothing else. That's my god, and nothing but money matters," he can get it, of course, but at what a cost! He is ignoring his obligation to lead a balanced life. We must also claim peace, harmony, beauty, guidance, love, joy, and wholeness in all phases of life.

To make money the sole aim in life would constitute an error or wrong choice. You must express your hidden talents, find your true place in life, and experience the joy of contributing to the growth, happiness and success of others. As you study this book and apply the laws of your subconscious in the right way, you can have all the money you want and still have peace of mind, harmony, wholeness, and serenity. To accumulate money to the exclusion of everything else causes a person to become lopsided and unbalanced.

I pointed out to this minister how he was completely misinterpreting the Scripture in pronouncing pieces of paper or metal evil. These were neutral substances. "There is nothing good or bad but thinking makes it so," I said. He began to think of all the good he could do for his wife, family, and parishioners if he had more money. He changed his attitude and let go of his superstition.

He began to claim boldly, regularly, and systematically

> **Infinite Spirit reveals better ways for me to serve. I am inspired and illumined, and I give a Divine transfusion of faith and confidence in the One Presence and Power to all those who hear me. I look upon money as God's idea, and it is constantly circulating in my life and that of my parishioners. We use it wisely, judiciously, and constructively under God's guidance and wisdom.**

This prayer activated the powers of his subconscious mind. Today the Rev. Edwin R. has a beautiful church that his congregation built for him and for themselves. His television broadcasts spread his teachings to millions of others. He has all the money he needs for his personal, worldly, and cultural needs. And I can assure you, he no longer criticizes money.

The Master Key and Program to Disciplining Your Mind for Money

If you follow the procedure and technique I am about to outline, you will never want for money all the days of your life.

1. Reason it out in your mind that God, or the Life-Principle, is the Source of the universe, the galaxies in space, and everything you see, whether you look at the stars in the sky, the mountains, the lakes, the deposits in the earth and sea, or all animals and plants. The Life-Principle gave birth to you, and all the powers, qualities, and attributes of God are within you. Ponder these truths:

- Everything you see or are aware of came out of the invisible mind of God, or Life.

- Everything that our species has invented, created, or made came out of the invisible mind of humankind.

- The mind of human and the mind of God are one, for there is only one mind common to all of us.

- God is the Source of your supply of energy, vitality, health, and creative ideas. God is the Source of the sun, the air you breathe, the apple you eat, and the money in your pocket.

- Everything comes of the Invisible. It is as easy for God to become wealth in your life as it is for Him to become a blade of grass.

2. Decide now to engrave in your subconscious mind the idea of wealth. Ideas are conveyed to the subconscious by repetition, faith, and expectancy. By repeating a thought pattern or an act over and over again, it becomes automatic. Because your subconscious is compulsive, you will be compelled to express it. There is no real difference between this process and learning to walk, swim, or play the piano. You must believe in what you are affirming. Realize that what you are affirming is like seeds you plant in the ground. They grow after their kind. By watering and fertilizing these seeds, you accelerate their growth. Know what you are doing and why you are doing it.

3. Repeat the following affirmation for five minutes night and morning:

> I am now writing in my subconscious mind the idea of God's wealth. God is the Source of my supply, and all my needs are met at every moment of time and point of space. God's wealth flows freely, joyously, and ceaselessly into my experience, and I give thanks for God's riches forever circulating in my experience.

4. When thoughts of lack come to you, such as, "I can't afford that trip" or "I can't pay that bill," never finish a negative statement about finances. Reverse it immediately in your mind by affirming, "God is my instant and everlasting supply, and that bill is paid in Divine order." If a negative thought comes to you 50 times in one hour, reverse it each time by thinking, "God is my instant supply, meeting that need right

now." After a while, the thought of financial lack will lose all momentum and you will find your subconscious is being conditioned to wealth. If you find yourself attracted to a new car, for example, never say, "I can't possibly afford that." On the contrary, say to yourself: "That car is for sale. It is a Divine idea, and I accept it in Divine Order."

This is the master key. When applied as outlined in the preceding program, the law of opulence will work for you, just as it does for others. The law of mind works equally for all. Your thoughts make you wealthy or poor. Choose the riches of life right here and right now.

A Sales Representative Is Stuck at $30,000 a Year

A sales manager sent me one of his employees for counseling. Rhoda G. was a brilliant college graduate and knew her products very well. She was in a lucrative territory but was making only about $30,000 annually in commissions. The sales manager felt she could easily double or triple that.

In talking to Rhoda, I found she was down on herself. She had been born into a family trapped by poverty. Her parents always took it for granted that she was destined to live in poverty just as they did. Instead of putting stress on the value of ambition, education, or hard work, they made fun of her aspirations for a better life. They told her she was getting ideas above her place in life. Her subconscious mind, especially impressionable in someone so young, accepted these imposed thoughts. Even when she chose an occupation that gave her the possibility of achieving her dreams, her subconscious belief in lack and limitation held her back.

I explained all this to Rhoda, then told her she could change her subconscious by feeding it with life-giving patterns. Accordingly, I gave her a mental and spiritual formula to follow that would transform her life. I stressed that she should under no circumstances deny what she affirmed, because her subconscious mind would accept and manifest what she really believed. Every morning before going to work, she affirmed

> I am born to succeed; the Infinite within me can't fail. Divine law and order govern my life, Divine peace fills my soul, Divine love saturates my mind. Infinite Intelligence guides me in all ways. God's riches flow to me freely. I am advancing, moving forward, and growing mentally, spiritually, financially, and in all other ways. I know these truths are sinking into my subconscious mind and will grow after their kind.

Her Subconscious Magnifies Her Earnings Greatly

A year later, I received a telephone call from Rhoda. She told me her life had been transformed as a result of the ideas we had discussed.

"I have learned to value myself," she said. "I am appreciating life now, and wonderful things have happened. My commissions over the last 12 months have amounted to almost $150,000. That's about five times what they were the year before. And last week my boss asked if I'd consider supervising sales in the entire southeastern district." As Rhoda realized, her success came as a result of learning the simple truth that whatever she inscribes in her subconscious mind becomes effective and functional in her life.

MEDITATION FOR A RICH HARVEST OF FINANCIAL WEALTH

Use the following meditation for assurance in achieving financial wealth:

> *Thou madest him to have dominion over the works of thy hands.* (Psalms 8:6) I know that my faith in God determines

my future. My faith in God means my faith in all things good. I unite myself now with true ideas, and I know the future will be in the image and likeness of my habitual thinking. *As a man thinketh in his heart so is he.* (Proverbs 23:7) From this moment forward my thoughts are on *Whatsoever things are true, whatsoever things are honest, whatsoever things are just, whatsoever things are lovely, and of good report* (Philippians 4:8); day and night I meditate on these things and I know these seeds, or thoughts, that I habitually dwell upon will become a rich harvest for me. I am the captain of my own soul; I am the master of my fate; for my thought and feeling are my destiny.

CHAPTER POINTS TO REMEMBER

1. Begin to think of the untold riches all around you waiting for the intelligence of humankind to reveal them. There is a guiding principle within you that, when called upon, will reveal to you the riches you are seeking.

2. There is an old saying: "Make friends with money, and you will always have it." Look upon money as God's idea, circulating among nations, maintaining economic health. Claim that money is circulating in your life, and your subconscious will see to it that you have all the money you need.

3. If you condemn money, calling it "filthy lucre," the root of all evil, and making other such nonsensical statements, your money will take wings and fly away. Money, like everything else in the universe, is universal substance, which is Spirit reduced to the point of visibility. Money, like nickel, cobalt, iron, platinum, lead, oil, and coal, are all forms of the universal substance operating at different frequencies and vibrations.

4. Adopt a new attitude toward money, realizing you are entitled to be richly compensated for your work, whether it be writing, teaching, gardening, or whatever. Think of

all the good you can do when money is circulating freely in your life.

5. You can work very hard, but if you dislike money or criticize it, you will find yourself in want financially. You do not make a god of money, but you realize that it is essential on this plane of existence. You look to the real Source of wealth, which is God, and you know that as you turn to the Source it will turn to you and give you all the riches of life. You do not worship a created thing, you worship the Creator. Your expectation is from God, who giveth to all life breath and all things richly to enjoy.

6. Claim that you are always using money wisely, judiciously, and constructively for your own good and for that of all men and women everywhere. Constantly claim also that the Infinite reveals better ways in which you can serve.

7. The master key to disciplining the mind for money is to come to a clear-cut decision once and for all that God is the source of everything you see in the universe and that everything people have made came also out of the mind of God. Believing this to be true, your affirmation for wealth will prove productive. When fearful thoughts or thoughts of lack come to your mind, reverse them at once by affirming, "God is my instant supply—that bill is paid in Divine mind now." Never finish a negative statement about your finances. After a while, the negative thoughts will cease to come, and you will find you have conditioned your subconscious to wealth.

8. A sales representative multiplied her income five times when she changed her attitude of mind about herself and money. Her subconscious belief in poverty had held her back. When she began to feed her subconscious mind with thoughts of success, opulence, right action, and abundance, she discovered that her thought, properly

guided, created promotion, wealth, self-esteem, and recognition from her superiors and customers. She learned that what she inscribes in her subconscious becomes effective and functional in her life. Her journey is now ever onward, upward, and Godward.

9. Use the meditation at the end of the chapter to assure yourself of a rich financial harvest.

How to Say the Exact Words That Will Bring You Money

Bring joy into your life! Pray for joy by claiming it. Affirm: "The joy of the Lord is my strength." Know that joy is the élan of life, the most basic expression of the Life-Force. Do not waste your time and energy analyzing the quest for joy or gritting your teeth and struggling to achieve it. No willpower or muscle power is needed for this mental and spiritual therapeutic technique, nor will they help. Just know and claim that the joy of the Lord is flowing through you now. Wonders will happen as you pray in this way. Freedom and peace of mind will be yours as a result.

How She Enriched Herself Through Effective Prayer

Carol B. came to me after one of my lectures and said, "I know that the techniques you're talking about work. They worked in my life."

"I'd like to hear about that," I replied.

"I'm divorced, with one kid, a second-grader," she said. "A few months ago I found myself at a total dead end financially. I was out of work, the bills were piling up, and when I looked in my wallet, all I had was $5. As I held it in my hand and stared at it, suddenly a great feeling of peace came over me. I was inspired to say, 'God will multiply this exceedingly, according to his riches in glory. I am now filled with the riches of God. My needs are met now and all the days my life.' The thought filled my mind for half an hour or more. I wasn't even aware of time passing. It was wonderful."

I was deeply impressed that this young woman had discovered such a powerful tool on her own. "What happened then?" I asked.

She smiled. "It was pretty amazing. Later that day, I went to the supermarket and spent the $5 on groceries. I didn't pay attention to the prices on what I bought, but at the checkout counter it came to exactly $5. I made a joke about it to the guy at the register, who turned out to be the store manager. He was tending the register because one of his cashiers had just quit unexpectedly. Well, the long and the short of it is, he asked me if I'd like the job. I accepted on the spot. Not only that, he and I get along really well. A few weeks ago we started dating. I have a feeling it is going to lead to something serious. I've gone from the real pits to experiencing all the riches of life."

Carol B. was moved to look to the Source. She believed in her heart, and the blessings of the Infinite followed. Her good was magnified and multiplied exceedingly.

How His Prayer for His Students Worked Wonders

On a flight to Hawaii, I got into a conversation with my seat mate. When I introduced myself and mentioned that I wrote inspirational books, his face lit up.

"You certainly do," he said. He explained that he taught Spanish and French in a church-affiliated school. Two years earlier, he had become so discouraged by the discipline problems and lack of progress among his students that he had seriously thought about giving up teaching and taking up a different profession. Then a friend of his suggested he read *The Power of Your Subconscious Mind.**

"The techniques you talked about made a lot of sense to me," he continued. "I decided to try adapting them to my own situation. I started asking my classes every morning to join together and affirm aloud: 'I am inspired from On High. Infinite Intelligence leads and guides me in my studies. I pass all my examinations in Divine order. I radiate love and goodwill to all my classmates. I am happy, joyous, and free. God loves me and cares for me.'"

"And what were the results?" I asked.

"Marvelous," he enthused. "I saw a tremendous change in my students. Since that time, not a single one has failed in my classes. What's more, they approach the work with a new enthusiasm. We now have very active Spanish and French Clubs for the first time in many years, and next fall I plan to organize student trips to Mexico and Quebec."

He added that he also tries to give his students a transfusion of faith and confidence in the Almighty by telling them every morning that they will pass, that they will be guided in their studies, and that they will have a perfect memory for everything they need to know. The students listen to him and absorb the truth of his statement. Together with their morning affirmations, these truths sink into their subconscious mind; and according to the impression in their subconscious, is it done unto them.

---

*The Power of Your Subconscious Mind by Joseph Murphy, revised and expanded by Ian McMahan. Paramus, NJ: Reward Books, 2000.

He is a wise teacher who has discovered that scientific prayer works wonders and miracles in an endless number of ways.

How Effective Prayer Enabled Them to Save His Job and Their Marriage

Bob and Donna J. came to me for help. They explained that I was their last hope as a couple. I spoke to them separately. Bob had a management position with a sizable construction firm, but he had just been fired because of excessive drinking on the job and because of an involvement with one of the women in the office. He was distressed, dejected, and worried about his wife, his income, and his future. He complained that his wife was very jealous and suspicious. She nagged him constantly and kept tabs on what time he came home every evening. If he was not in by a certain hour, she made a scene.

"But wasn't she right to be jealous?" I asked him. "You *were* having an affair, after all."

"She was that way before the affair," he retorted. "I think I got involved with Sally just to get even with Donna and prove that I couldn't be penned in."

When I talked with Donna, she admitted she had a problem with jealousy. "I keep feeling that Bob is slipping away from me," she said. "Even when he's home, he's not all the way there. And the harder I try to pin him down, the more he wriggles away."

I explained to them that the way each of them was acting sent the wrong messages to the other's subconscious mind. The result was that their problems got steadily worse. The path to a solution would involve breaking out of this vicious circle by beginning to send a different, more constructive message to their subconscious mind.

At my suggestion, they committed themselves to praying night and morning. They realized that as they prayed for each other, they would begin to dissolve all bitterness, hostility, and resentment, for Divine love casts out everything unlike itself.

Donna prayed night and morning as follows:

> **My husband is God's child. God is guiding him to his true place. What he is seeking is seeking him. God's love fills his soul and God's peace fills his mind and heart. God prospers him in all ways. There are harmony, peace, love, and understanding between us. It is God in action in our lives.**

At the same time, Bob prayed for his wife night and morning as follows:

> **My wife is God's child. God loves her and cares for her. God's love, peace, harmony, and joy flow through her at all times and she is Divinely guided in all ways. There are harmony, peace, love, and understanding between us. I see God in her, and she sees God in me.**

How It All Worked Out

As Donna and Bob continued to pray for each other, they became more relaxed and confident about their relationship. Their financial situation, however, was still a matter of deep concern. Then Bob got a phone call from his former superior at the construction company, who praised his past achievements and accomplishments for the organization and asked if he would be willing to return to his old job. Of course, Bob agreed.

Later, Donna told Bob that she had called and spoken to his ex-boss. She had told him that she and Bob were rebuilding their marriage and that Bob was no longer drinking. She had also said that they were now praying together and explained how and why. Bob's superior was deeply impressed.

He said he was sure Bob would become an even more valuable employee than before he began to have problems. The miraculous power of scientific prayer had preserved their relationship and rebuilt his career, both on a more secure foundation.

Let the Riches of the Infinite Flow Through You

Constantly affirm, feel, and believe that God multiplies your good exceedingly. You will be enriched every moment of the day spiritually, mentally, intellectually, financially, and socially. There is no end to the glory of man for his daily living. Watch the wonders that will happen as you impress these truths on your subconscious mind. You will experience a glorious future.

The Sure Riches of "Watch and Pray"

Watch your thoughts. Never talk about economic lack and limitation, never talk about being poor or in want. It is especially foolish to talk to your neighbors or relatives about hard times or financial problems. Count your blessings. Begin to think prosperous thoughts. Talk about God's riches, present everywhere. Realize that the feeling of wealth produces wealth. When you talk about not having enough to go around, and how little you have, and how you must cut corners, these thoughts are creative. They bring about the conditions you are describing. You are only impoverishing yourself.

Use the money you now have freely. Release it with joy and realize that God's wealth flows to you in avalanches of abundance. Look up to the Source. As you turn to God, the response will come, as "He careth for you." You will find neighbors, strangers, and associates adding to your good and also to your supply of material things. Make it a practice to pray for Divine guidance in all your ways and believe that God is supplying all your needs according to His riches in glory. As you make a habit of this attitude of mind, you will find the invisible law of opulence can and will produce visible riches for you.

She Became a Tremendous Success Through Effective Prayer

Samantha G. is the owner of a thriving beauty salon. She told me the secret of her success. Every morning, before opening for business, she has a quiet period in which she affirms

> God's peace fills my soul, and God's love saturates my whole being. God guides, prospers, and inspires me. I am illumined, and His healing love flows from me to all my clients. Divine love comes in my door and Divine love goes out of my door. All those who come into my salon are blessed, healed, and inspired. The Infinite Healing Presence saturates the whole place. This is the day the Lord hath made, and I rejoice and give thanks for the countless blessings that come to my clients and myself.

She wrote out this prayer on a card and reiterates these truths every morning. At night she gives thanks for all her clients, claiming that they are guided, prospered, happy, and harmonious and that God and His love flow through each one, filling up all the empty vessels in her life.

She went on to say that three months after beginning to use this prayer technique, she had far more clients than she could handle. She had to hire three more beauticians. Now she is making plans to open a day spa in an adjoining building.

She has discovered the riches of effective prayer and is prospering beyond her fondest dreams.

Realize the Rich Blessings of the Infinite

Recently Dr. Belinda C., a pediatrician in Beverly Hills, said to me, "I live in the joyous expectation of the best, and invariably the best comes to me. I saturate my mind with my favorite Bible verse, *He giveth to all life, and breath, and all things* (Acts 17:25). I've learned that I am not dependent on people for joy, health, success, happiness, or peace of mind."

Dr. C. looks to the Living Spirit Almighty within her for promotion, achievement, wealth, success, and happiness. *Whosoever trusteth in the Lord, happy is he* (Proverbs 16:20).

Contemplate promotion, success, achievement, illumination, and inspiration, and the Spirit of the Almighty will move on your behalf. It will compel you to express fully what you meditate on. Let go now, and permit the Infinite riches of the Infinite One to open up new doors for you. Let wonders happen in your life.

The Riches of Effective Prayer Therapy

In prayer therapy, avoid struggle and strain. These are really signs of your unbelief. In your subconscious is all the wisdom and power necessary to solve any problem. Your conscious mind is prone to look at external conditions and tends continually to struggle and to resist. Remember, however, it is the quiet mind that gets things done. Quiet your body periodically; tell it to be still and relax, and it will obey you. When your conscious mind is quiet and receptive, the wisdom of your subconscious mind rises to the surface and you receive your solution.

How Do You Feel After Prayer?

You can know if you have succeeded in prayer by the way you feel. If you remain worried or anxious, and if you are wondering how, when, where, or through what source your answer will come, you are meddling. You do not really trust the wisdom of your subconscious. Avoid nagging yourself all day long, or even from time to time. When you think of your desire, lightness of touch is terribly important. Remind yourself that Infinite Intelligence is taking care of the problem in Divine order, and far better than you could do by the tense efforts of your conscious mind.

How Often Should You Pray?

People frequently ask me, "How often should I pray for a loved one who is ill, who is in the hospital, or who is having serious financial problems?" The best response I can give is that you should pray until you feel satisfied within, or until you feel that this is the best you can do for the time being. Expect your prayer for harmony, wholeness, vitality, and abundance to be answered. You may pray later on during the day, as the spirit moves you. You will know when your prayer is answered, because you will experience an inner sense of peace and certitude.

Long sessions of prayer are usually a mistake. They may indicate that you are trying to force things by using mental coercion. This generally leads to the opposite of what you are praying for. You will often find that a short prayer uttered from the heart gets better results than a long prayer.

He Restoreth My Soul (Psalm 23:3)

Learn to let go and relax. Do not give power to the ailment or condition. Give power and allegiance to the Infinite Healing Presence. The swimming instructor tells you that you can float on the water, which will support you if you remain quiet, still, and at peace. But if you get nervous or fearful, you will sink.

When you are seeking a spiritual healing, feel that you are immersed in the Holy Omnipresence. Know that the golden river of life, love, truth, and beauty is flowing through you, transforming your whole being into the pattern of harmony, health, and peace. Identify yourself with the river of life and love. Feel yourself swimming in the great ocean of life. That sense of oneness with God will restore you. *He restoreth my soul* (Psalm 23:3).

MEDITATION FOR A WONDERFUL FUTURE

The following meditation used daily will bring you many wonderful things:

> I know that I mold, fashion, and create my own destiny. My faith in God is my destiny. I cherish an abiding faith in all things good. I live in the joyous expectancy of the best; only the best comes to me. I know the harvest I will reap in the future, because all my thoughts are God's thoughts, and God is with my thoughts of good. My thoughts are the seeds of goodness, truth, and beauty. I now place my thoughts of love, peace, joy, success, and goodwill in the garden of my mind. This is God's garden, and it will yield an abundant harvest. The glory and beauty of God will be expressed in my life. From this moment forward, I express life, love, and truth. I am radiantly happy and prosperous in all ways. Thank you, Father.

☞ CHAPTER POINTS TO REMEMBER ☜

1. Whatever money you have, bless it now and believe it when you say, "God will multiply this exceedingly, now

and forevermore." Believe it in your heart and you will never want all the days of your life.

2. When a husband and wife pray for each other, exalting the presence of God in one another and claiming peace, harmony, love, and inspiration, all resentment and ill will are dissolved, and both will prosper. If you are fired from a position, claim, "Only good can come out of this." You will discover a new door that opens up a far more wonderful position than the previous one.

3. Focus your attention on whatsoever things are lovely, noble, wonderful and God-like, and you will experience the riches of life. Remember, you reap what you sow in your subconscious.

4. Watch your thoughts. Your thoughts are creative. Never talk about lack, limitation, or being unable to make ends meet. This multiplies your misery. Think of God's riches. Affirm boldly that the riches of the Infinite are flowing to you in avalanches of abundance. Claim it boldly and the Infinite will respond.

5. The owner of a beauty salon became an outstanding success by affirming regularly and systematically: "God's peace fills my soul, and God's love saturates my whole being. His healing love flows from me to all my clients. All those who come into my salon are blessed, healed, prospered, and inspired." She made a habit of this prayer and has prospered beyond her fondest dreams.

6. A wonderful prayer enabling you to experience the riches of the Infinite is this: "I live in the joyous expectancy of the best and invariably the best comes to me. *God giveth to all life, and breath, and all things* (Acts 17:25)."

7. In teaching students, realize that Infinite Intelligence is guiding and directing them in their studies. Claim that

they pass all their examinations in Divine order. Give them a transfusion of faith and confidence in the Power within them, and you will be amazed how they pick up your conviction of them subconsciously. Wonders happen as you pray this way.

8. Assure yourself of a full, rich future by using the meditation at the end of the chapter.

How to Activate the Psychic Money Machine

"To prosper" means not just to succeed, but to *thrive*. When you prosper, you expand. You grow spiritually, mentally, financially, socially, and intellectually. In order to truly prosper, you must become a channel through which the Life-Principle flows freely, harmoniously, joyously, and lovingly. If you sincerely want to achieve this, I suggest that you establish a definite method of working and thinking and that you practice it regularly and systematically every day.

How Prosperity Thoughts Changed His Life

"I've prayed for prosperity constantly, for years," James V. told me tonelessly. "It's all nonsense. I'm as poor as ever, and that's all I can ever expect."

"You feel your prayers have not been answered," I said.

"You got it," he replied. "I just hope my situation doesn't get even worse than it already is. I'm in hock up to my ears. I wake up at night worrying about how I'll ever get out of this."

James explained that he had worked his way through law school and specialized in oil and gas law. When international developments led to a severe cutback in domestic oil exploration, the corporation where he worked slashed its personnel, including the legal department. As one of the newer lawyers, he was the first to get the boot. Since then, he had had only occasional, temporary positions.

"I don't know why I'm even wasting your time," he added. "Even if my prayers worked, how can they have any effect on what OPEC does next? I'm toast."

"Let me explain something," I suggested. "You say you've prayed for prosperity, and I'm sure you have. But you've spent much more of your time worrying about poverty and failure. If you present your subconscious mind with two conflicting ideas, it accepts the dominant one. Your fear of poverty *attracts* lack and limitation."

"You mean my own thoughts are the reason for my situation?" he said dubiously.

"Exactly," I said. "Every thought is creative unless it is neutralized by a counter thought of greater intensity. Your thoughts and beliefs about poverty have been much stronger than your belief in the infinite riches all around you. When you visualize poverty, you help *create* poverty. And if you begin to visualize wealth, you will produce wealth."

By the end of our conversation, James had made a firm decision to change his thinking. At his request, I wrote out a prosperity prayer for him and urged him to meditate on it first thing each morning and last thing each night.

An Effective Prosperity Prayer

This is the prayer I wrote for James:

I know there is only one Source, the Life-Principle, from which all things flow. It created the universe and all things therein contained. I am a focal point of the Divine presence. My mind is open and receptive. I am a free-flowing channel for harmony, beauty, guidance, wealth, and the riches of the Infinite. I know that health, wealth, and success are released, from within and appear without. I am now in harmony with the infinite riches within and without, and I know these thoughts are sinking into my subconscious mind and will be reflected on the screen of space. I wish for everyone all the blessings of life. I am open and receptive to God's riches—spiritual, mental, and material—and they flow to me in avalanches of abundance.

His Changed Thinking Suddenly Changed Him into a Prosperous Person

James V. diligently focused his thoughts on God's riches rather than on poverty. He made it a special point not to deny what he affirmed by worrying about his financial situation. For 10 minutes every morning and evening, he affirmed the truths expressed in his prosperity prayer. He knew that by doing so he was actually inscribing these truths in his subconscious mind and encouraging it to become active and release its hidden treasures.

A month later, I received a letter from him. Here is an excerpt:

> Last week I went to a free concert in the park. I accepted the music joyously as a gift, instead of brooding over the fact that I couldn't have afforded to buy a ticket. During the intermission, I got into a conversation with a couple sitting near me. They were from out of town, and I was able to give them some tips about restaurants and shops. When they learned my profession, the woman, Joan, said, "I do believe this was meant to be!"

> She told me that she and her husband were independent operators—what used to be called wildcatters. They had decided to expand into my state, and their first priority was to find an attorney who knew all the ins and outs of local oil and gas laws. After the concert, they took me to dinner at a fine restaurant. Before the meal was over, we'd agreed that I would

come to work for them, for a significantly higher salary than my last job *and* a participation in my division's earnings. It is a dream come true!

How She Wrote Her Desires in Her Prayerful Heart

A young woman came to me after one of my public lectures. She introduced herself as Betty S. and said excitedly, "Such a wonderful idea came to me while you were speaking. I suddenly saw my conscious mind as an indelible pen. The more I use it to think about what I really want, the more clearly my desire gets written on my subconscious mind. Then my subconscious gets busy making it come true. Is that right?"

"That's exactly right," I told her, smiling at her enthusiasm. "You have the power to inscribe your true desires on your subconscious by frequently devoting your mind to the desires of your heart."

"I'm going to do it!" Betty exclaimed, snapping her fingers. "There are two things I really want, so I'll think of each of them separately. Then it's up to my subconscious to bring them about in the best way it can. I know it'll work!"

Her Most Cherished Desires

I asked Betty if she was willing to tell me her two desires.

"Oh, sure," she replied. "The first one is to take my mother on a vacation to Mexico. She's always wanted to visit Mexico, but she never had the chance."

"And the second one?" I asked.

She hesitated, and her face turned pink. "I want to meet someone, fall in love, and get married."

I smiled. "Let's see how your subconscious handles that."

We discussed how she would approach inscribing her two desires. For the first one, she decided that she and her mother would both visualize themselves packing, boarding the plane, arriving in Mexico, and exploring the picturesque streets of the town they were visiting. As they did so, both separately and together, they would repeat the thought, "Infinite Intelligence opens up the way in Divine order."

Three weeks later, Betty showed up at my office all excited. "You're not going to believe this," she said. "Some kid came by last week selling raffle tickets to benefit the local community center. I bought a book of five. Well, the drawing was last night, and my ticket was one of the winners. Guess what my prize was?"

I took a chance. "A trip for two to Mexico?"

Betty stared at me. "How on earth did you guess? When they told me, I almost fainted! Is that weird, or what?"

"No," I replied. "It's amazing, but it's not weird. Your subconscious has ways to get results that are truly past finding out. Accept it, and rejoice in it."

For Betty's second desire, she used her conscious mind pen to write this thought in her subconscious:

> I know my desire for marriage and happiness is the voice of God in me urging me to lead a full and happy life. I know that I am one with the Infinite now. I know and believe there is a man waiting to love and cherish me. I know I can contribute to his happiness and peace. I can be a great asset to him. I can cherish, love, and inspire him to greatness, just as he inspires me. He loves my ideals, and I love his ideals. He does not want to make me over; neither do I want to make him over. There are mutual love, freedom, and respect between us. These words go forth and accomplish whereunto they are sent. I have written this request in my subconscious mind with faith and confidence, and I decree it is done, finished, and established in my deeper mind. Whenever I think of marriage, I shall remind myself that the Infinite Intelligence of my subconscious is bringing this to pass in Divine order.

A few weeks later, she needed some dental work. Her appointment was the dentist's last of the day. Afterwards, they got into a conversation. When Betty told him about her trip to Mexico, he asked her to join him for dinner at his favorite

Mexican restaurant. Their interest in each other deepened. Some time later, I had the joy and satisfaction of performing their marriage ceremony. Betty S. achieved her desires through her insight into the wonders of her subconscious mind. Think prosperous and wholesome thoughts, and wonders happen as you pray.

How Riches of Daily Healthy Thinking Brought Great Benefits

Richard M., a software engineer, came to consult me. He told me he was recently divorced. "My own fault, I guess," he added. "I'm just not very interesting. Neither is my life. I go to work, I go to the gym, I go to sleep. Then I get up the next day and do it again. Why would anybody want to share that, or even hear about it? That must be why I don't have any friends—I bored them all to death."

"Suppose you were trying to analyze a computer program," I said. "If you saw that every time it produced a certain message, the result was always the same, what would you think?"

He rubbed his ear and said, "First approximation, the message is causing the result. So I'd try altering the message and see if the result changed."

"Good," I said. "I'd like you to consider the idea that your thoughts are creative. When you tell yourself you are boring and friendless, your negative thoughts actually compound the problem. Whatever we give attention to, the subconscious magnifies and multiplies in our experience."

"I get it," he said. "You're saying if I reverse my thinking, I'll get a different result. I'm game. What do I do next?"

I suggested he affirm frequently and systematically:

> I am happy, joyous and free. I am loving, kind, harmonious and peaceful. I sing the song of praise in the Lord, which is my strength.

He realized and understood the mental law that whatever he attached to the thought *I am . . .* he would manifest and express. He made a habit of affirming these mental truths, and his whole life changed. From what had seemed a drab, lonely existence, he went to a full, rich life, with new interests, new friends, new close relationships, and a new insight into the wonders of the riches within him.

How She Planned for Prosperity and Happiness and Got Results

"I'm not complaining, you understand," Claire R. told me earnestly. She had just told me that her husband had a good job with the telephone company. They had two young children, whom Claire stayed home and cared for. "All the same, I feel stuck on a treadmill. Every day the same thing—cook, wash up, do the laundry, shop, think of stuff for the kids to do . . . I'm always tired, and my mind doesn't work the way it used to. It's as if a spark has gone out."

"You feel that life is against you?" I asked.

"That's it," she agreed. "Well, not against me exactly, but passing me by."

I explained that her thought-images about her condition were helping to create the very conditions that made her unhappy. "An emotionally impoverished life is a state of mind," I continued. "So are happiness and prosperity. If you can learn to reverse your way of thinking, you will see a real, dramatic effect in your life."

She began to claim, twice every day:

> Divine right action is mine. Success is mine. Wealth is mine. Happiness is mine. God's river of peace flows through my mind, body, and activities, and whatever I do will prosper. I know my thoughts are creative. As an engineer plans a bridge, so am I planning prosperity and happiness now. I believe implicitly in the law of the Bible, which promises, *Ask, and it*

*shall be given you; seek, and ye shall find; knock, and it shall
be opened unto you* (Matthew 7:7).

In this way, Claire R. stirred up the gift of God's prosperity within herself. Her relationship to her home, her marriage, and her children changed. She released the imprisoned splendors within. Money came in from totally unexpected sources, and she became completely satisfied with her new lot in life.

There Are Beauty and Abundance Where You Are

God is indescribable beauty, and God indwells you. He walks and talks in you. Your mind and your spirit, your thoughts and your feelings all represent God within you. The invisible life and power within you is God. Your thought, being creative, is God in action in your life. Begin to contemplate that God's beauty and riches flow through your thoughts, words, and deeds, and you will pass on the beauty and riches of God to your family, friends, and neighbors. Give thanks for all the blessings you have. You can make your home beautiful and you can inspire others to experience the riches of your deeper mind. You are the artist, the weaver, the designer, and the architect of your life.

The Riches of His Secret Plan for Making a Profitable Business Deal

For years I shopped at a specialty market near my home. It was a family-owned business, now run by the third generation. I had a nodding acquaintance with the two brothers who owned it, and I was sad to hear that one of them died. A few weeks later, the surviving brother, Vincent M., came over and asked if he could talk with me. He explained that his brother had left his half-interest in the business to his two children, Vincent's nieces.

"I don't know why," he said. "I love them like my own children, but they are making such problems for me. One demand after another. Everything I propose, they are against. We have some important decisions to make soon, and I'm afraid it's going to be a deadlock. I know family businesses that went under, had to liquidate, because of this kind of problem. I don't want ours to be one of them."

"Are you in a position to buy them out?" I asked.

"It wouldn't be easy, but I could swing it," he replied. "I offered. No deal. They acted insulted that I'd even suggested it. I'm at my wits' end on this."

"You have to let it go," I urged him. "The negative energy created by your worries is part of what's creating the problem."

With some help from me, Vincent wrote the following on a piece of paper:

> **I loose my nieces to God completely. They are in their true place. They are inspired to right action in Divine order. Nothing is forever. This condition passes away now. It is God in action.**

He put the paper in a file folder labeled, *With God all things are possible,* stuck it in his desk drawer, and forgot about it. In two weeks' time, his nieces came to him. They had realized that their late father would have wanted them to do what was best for the store. They agreed to sell their interest at a fair price. Everyone was satisfied, and harmony was restored to both the business and the family.

The technique Vincent used was sound. When he wrote down his desired outcome, he was actually inscribing it in his subconscious mind. The act of placing it in a drawer in his desk was simply an outer symbol. He released his problem to the Infinite Intelligence of his subconscious mind, which is the secret place from which you draw forth the answer to all your problems.

How to Consider the Riches of the Infinite

The blue sky by day and the stars by night are there for you as for everyone. You can admire the sunset whether you are rich or poor. You can listen to the songs of the birds and become enraptured with the beauty all around you. Begin to see the Divine presence in all things about you—in the rising sun, the golden moon, the sky, the mountains, the rivers, the rivulets, and the streams. Contemplate the beauty of all nature. Love surrounds you.

Life is a mirror that reflects back to us precisely what we deposit in our minds. Look through the eyes of love and beauty, and love, beauty, and the riches of the Infinite will come back to you. Longfellow said, "Look not mournfully into the past; it comes not back again. Wisely improve the present; it is the thing. Go forth to meet the shadowy future without fear and a manly heart." Seneca said, "We can only say he is anxious about the future to whom the present is unprofitable." God (your good) is the Eternal now! Claim your good and all the riches of life now. What you can conceive, you can achieve, through the wisdom and power of your subconscious mind.

The Wonders of Prosperous and Healthy Writing Out of Your Desires

Every New Year's Eve, I conduct a New Year's prayer for the same group of men and women. We have a custom at these events: Each person writes out clearly his or her desires of the heart. We use only four categories: health, wealth, love, and expression. No matter what you seek comes under one of these classifications. If, for example, you request wisdom as your sole desire, that comes under expression, or your desire to release more and more of the life, love, truth, beauty, and riches of the deeper mind. I suggest that, when writing down their desires, the participants include a wish for a friend or relative. For example, if the friend or relative had family difficulties, they were instructed to write down: "There is a Divine and harmonious solution through the infinite justice and harmony of God for _____."

How Desires Written Out Have Come to Be Fulfilled

After everyone has written out his or her requests, they are placed in sealed envelopes and given to one of the participants, who stores them in a safe at home. The following New Year's Eve, each person is given his or her envelope to open and read privately.

It amazes everyone to see how many of these desires have been answered during the year just past. One man showed me his request. His most important desire had been to have more time for his wife and children. Another request had been to travel with his family. During the course of the year, his company promoted him and transferred him to another part of the country. He was given six weeks off for the transition and used them to take a long cruise with his family. In his new job, he was living much closer to work and had more time at home every day.

These men and women write down the deepest desires of their hearts, trusting and believing that the Infinite Intelligence in their subconscious mind will bring their desires to pass in Divine order. I always conclude my annual prayer with the group in this way:

> **We decree that all these written desires are inscribed in the subconscious of each and that all these desires come forth in Divine law and order.**

The Real Secret of It All

The secret purpose of writing these desires and sealing them is that we release them completely to the wisdom of the subconscious with faith and confidence. We know that, just as the sun rises in the morning, so will there be a resurrection of all these desires in Divine order. This is called Divine indifference. When you have this attitude of mind, your prayers are always answered. Divine indifference means that you know it is impossible for your prayer to fail, for it is written, *He will not fail thee, nor forsake thee* (Deuteronomy 31:6)

MEDITATION FOR IMPREGNATING YOUR SUBCONSCIOUS MIND

The following meditation, sincerely believed and repeated often, will yield you great treasures:

> *Be ye doers of the word, and not hearers only, deceiving yourselves.* (James 1:22) My creative word is my silent conviction that my prayer is answered. When I speak the word for healing, success, or prosperity, my word is spoken in the consciousness of life and power, knowing that it is done. My word has power, because it is one with omnipotence. The words I speak are always constructive and creative. When I pray, my words are full of life, love, and feeling. This makes my affirmations, thoughts, and words creative. I know the greater my faith behind the word spoken, the more power it has. The words I use form a definite mold that determines what form my thought is to take. Divine intelligence operates through me now and reveals to me what I need to know. I have the answer now. I am at peace. God is Peace.

☞ CHAPTER POINTS TO REMEMBER ☞

1. You are prospering when you are expanding along all lines spiritually, mentally, intellectually, and financially. You should have all the money you need to do what you want to do, when you want to do it.

2. Your subconscious mind accepts the dominant of two ideas. Reason out clearly all the reasons why all things visible and invisible come from one Source. All things

made by humankind came out of the one mind, and all things made by God came out of the same mind. Think prosperity thoughts. Think of riches of all kinds and the immense wealth of the world, and your subconscious will respond to your habitual thinking. Supplant all thoughts of poverty with the thought of God's opulence and endless resources. Be open and receptive, and let wealth flow freely to you. Be a good receiver.

3. Your conscious mind is the pen with which you inscribe your true desires in your subconscious. Think quietly and with interest of each desire separately, watering it and nurturing it with faith and expectancy. Do this three or four times a day. By frequent habitation of the mind, you will impregnate your subconscious, and the cherished desires of your heart will be realized.

4. Never engage in thinking of lack, limitation, loneliness, and frustration. On the contrary, have a mental plan of the things you want, and then realize that whatever you attach to *I am . . . ,* you will create in your life. Get a little phrase easily graven on the memory, such as "I am happy, joyous, and free." Repeat it over and over again as a lullaby. Do it knowingly and feelingly. As you sow in your subconscious, so also will you reap.

5. Instead of grumbling, whining, and complaining about current conditions, reverse that attitude of mind and claim boldly: "Divine right action is mine. Divine success is mine. Divine love fills my soul, and whatever I do will prosper." Know that your thoughts are creative and that you are what you think all day long. Have a healthy respect for your thoughts. Your thought is your prayer.

6. Begin to contemplate that God's beauty and riches flow freely through your thoughts, words, and deeds and you will experience the results of your thinking; furthermore, you will be able to pass on to your family the riches

acquired by contemplation. You must have in order to give. Only rich people can contribute richly to all; the poor cannot give.

7. When you are in a quandary and are dealing with difficult people, it is a good thing to write out clearly your desire, as follows: "This, too, will pass away. There is a Divine and harmonious solution through the wisdom of my subconscious. I loose it and let it go now." Put this written prayer in a folder marked "With God all things are possible." This is a symbolic way of releasing it, and it works wonders.

8. Life is a mirror for the king and the beggar, reflecting back to each of us precisely that which we deposit in our mind.

9. I have conducted group prayers on New Year's Eve where each person writes out his or her heart's desires. These prayers are sealed in an envelope, locked away for one year, and opened the following New Year's Eve. All the members are amazed at the way their prayers were answered. Many had forgotten what they wrote and were astounded. The secret is that they released all their prayers with faith and confidence to the deeper mind, which knows all and sees all. They learned that when one has a Divine indifference, the prayer is always answered. Divine indifference is not carelessness or apathy; rather, it means that you know whatever you claim and feel to be true in your heart must come to pass. Therefore, you wait for the answer with greater faith, assurance, and conviction than the person who waits for the coming of the dawn.

10. The meditation at the end of the chapter will yield you amazing benefits for daily living.

How to Make and Use a Psychic Treasure Map

The soul without imagination is what an observatory would be without a telescope.

HENRY WARD BEECHER

Imagination disposes of everything; it creates beauty, justice, and happiness, which are everything in this world.

BLAISE PASCAL

The poet's eye, in a fine frenzy rolling, doth glance from heaven to earth, from earth to heaven; and as imagination bodies forth the forms of things unknown, the poet's pen turns them to shape, and gives to airy nothing a local habitation and a name, such tricks had strong imagination.

WILLIAM SHAKESPEARE

Imagination is one of our most powerful faculties. Disciplined, controlled, and directed imagination is a mighty instrument that plumbs the depths of your subconscious mind, bringing forth new inventions, discoveries, poems, music, and an awareness of the riches of the air, the sea, and the earth. Scientists, artists, musicians, physicists, inventors, poets, and writers generally possess highly developed imaginative faculties, which draw forth from the treasure house of their subconscious the riches of the Infinite and bless humankind in countless ways.

How Her Treasure Map Brought Her Riches and Companionship

Recently I performed a marriage ceremony for a young woman named Amanda R. I had first met Amanda, an account executive with a public relations firm, about six months earlier. She was concerned that her firm was in difficulties and that her life was not developing in the direction she would like. After our conversation, she drew up for herself a treasure map. It was divided into four parts. In the first section, she wrote, "I give thanks for God's wealth flowing freely in my life." In the second, she wrote, "I give thanks for a trip around the world." In the third, she wrote, "I give thanks for a wonderful, spiritual-minded man who harmonizes with me perfectly." In the last, she wrote, "I give thanks for a beautiful, harmonious home." Under these four requests, she wrote, "I give thanks for the immediate fulfillment of all these requests in Divine order through Divine love."

Every morning, afternoon, and evening she contemplated her requests. She affirmed and visualized their fulfillment as vividly as possible. She knew that gradually these images would be written in her subconscious mind, which would bring them to pass. The answer to her first request came in about a month's time. Her great-aunt in New York bequeathed over $150,000 worth of securities to her in her will. Two days after her firm closed, putting her out of work, her parents in Canada invited her to take a trip with them around the world. While in Tokyo, she met a young scientist from near San Francisco. As she said, it was love at first sight. Their marriage took place on their return to California. They are now living in his beautiful hillside home with a magnificent view of the Pacific Ocean.

Amanda told me that she never doubted writing out a treasure map would work. She implicitly trusted the Infinite Intelligence of her subconscious mind. To aid her in her visualizations, she obtained a passport, selected a tour from a travel brochure, and focused each night on a different foreign city she planned to visit. She also visualized a ring on her finger, which meant to her that she was already married to a wonderful man.

Amanda's method helped her gain control over her thinking and imagination. This enabled her to have dominion over her financial affairs, while at the same time bringing fulfillment in her love life and the field of expression.

His Imagination Brought About a Legal Settlement

I was on a visit to Yucatan, to tour the ruins of Chichen Itza, center of the ancient Mayan civilization, when I met an attorney from Texas named Doug M. As we talked, he confided that this vacation was likely to be the last peaceful moment for him for quite a while. Waiting for him back in Dallas was a case that involved a very large estate and a number of quarrelling relatives of the deceased. He had been engaged by one member of the family who hoped to bring peace and harmony and avoid a long, expensive lawsuit.

"I'd have better luck marrying a coonhound to a wildcat than getting that ornery bunch to agree on anything," he said despairingly.

"I have a suggestion," I replied. "Give imaginative prayer therapy a try. Project yourself mentally into your firm's conference room in Dallas. All the members of the family are there. Now, claim with complete faith that harmony, peace, and understanding operate among them. Imagine your client telling you, 'We have agreed to respect the terms of the will as written and not to contest it in court.' Do that every night at bedtime, then lull yourself to sleep with the words, 'Happy ending.'"

Doug seemed intrigued by my suggestion. "I am ready to try anything," he said.

When I returned from Mexico, I found a letter waiting, postmarked Dallas. In it, Doug wrote:

> I tried prayer therapy, as you suggested. When the family conference came along, I walked in secure in my conviction of a harmonious solution. Sure enough, the most contentious family members had thought it over and decided to abide by the will. We avoided a nasty court battle, and I might add, I received a handsome fee as well as everybody's thanks.

How a Mexican Guide Uses His Imagination in His Other Career

Uxmal is one of the major archaeological sites in Mexico. It lies on the Merida-Campeche highway, slightly over an hour by car from the capital of Yucatan. The guide who drove me there was named Porfirio G. He told me that his real calling, which he exercises mostly during quiet periods when there are not so many tourists, is that of dowser and water diviner. When a landowner asks him to find water, he visits the ranch and walks around holding a bent piece of copper wire. As he covers the territory, he talks to his arm, saying, "You will get firm and rigid when we are near water. The copper wire will point to the exact spot where the water is."

"It almost always works," Porfirio added. "When I fail, it is because I am tired and I do not concentrate enough."

Porfirio took several very detailed topographic maps from the door pocket of the car. "I can dowse with these, too," he said. "When a *ranchero* has lost some cattle, I think very hard about the lost animals. Then I pass the copper rod over the map and it tells me where they may be."

Porfirio's income from dowsing has allowed him to work toward a degree at the local university. He hopes soon to be appointed an instructor in archeology.

"All of the Yucatan is rich in Mayan ruins that have been covered over by the jungle," he said excitedly. "I intend to search for them with my copper wire. And I am sure I will find them, just as I find water and lost cattle. One day all the world will marvel at the achievements of our distant ancestors."

He Was Tapping the Riches Already in His Subconscious

When Porfirio was still a child, his father told him that he had inherited the gift of dowsing. The boy believed him. Because the subconscious is amenable to suggestion and is controlled by suggestion, his subconscious responded according to his belief. The subconscious mind is coextensive with all wisdom and intelligence. It sees all and knows all. It knows where water is, or gold, or lost livestock, or ancient ruins, for the whole world came out of the universal subconscious.

When Porfirio walks in an area where water is, his belief and his definite command to his subconscious mind bring about a constriction of the muscles of his arm that causes the wire to point to the spot to dig. The wire is nothing more than an encouraging prop. He could just as effectively use a tree limb, a crystal on a string, or anything else he believes will work.

I complimented Porfirio on his dedication and wished him all success. I also suggested that he might improve his technique by frequently telling his subconscious mind, "When I reach the spot, I will know exactly how many feet deep the source of water is." *According to his belief is it done unto him.*

The Law of Constructive Imagining Overcame Her Discouragement

I first met Virginia B. a few years ago. At that time she was a successful media buyer for an advertising agency and happily married to an attorney. The next time we met, she was depressed, dejected, and discouraged. She told me her husband had suffered a fatal stroke a year earlier, shortly after she retired from her agency. Since then, she had been trying, without any success, to sell her house. The upkeep and expenses of it were too much for her to handle. She had put down a binder on a charming apartment in a nearby retirement community, but unless she could find a buyer for her house very quickly, she would lose the apartment and forfeit her deposit.

I told Virginia she should put her imagination to work and explained how to do it. Each night, before going to sleep, she should imagine a check in her hand for the full price of her home. In her controlled imagination, she would deposit it in the bank with a great feeling of inner satisfaction. After this, she was to visualize, as vividly and concretely as possible, going to her new apartment and getting ready for bed. As she drifted off to sleep in her new bedroom, she was to say, "Thank you, Father, for the fulfillment of my prayer in Divine order."

Virginia followed this procedure for three consecutive nights. On the morning of the fourth day, the realtor who was listing her home called her. An executive who had just been transferred from the East Coast was looking for something just like her house and needed to close a deal immediately. The broker and the prospective buyer came over an hour later. By midafternoon, the sale had been concluded.

Truly, imagination has been called the workshop of God. Einstein said, "Imagination is greater than knowledge." What you can imagine and feel to be true will come to pass. Imagination clothes your ideas and projects them on the screen of space. Be faithful to the mental image in your mind and you will find it one day manifested in reality.

How an Actress's Imagination Overcame Her Sense of Frustrating Competition

Mona V. is a beautiful and talented actress, but when I met her she had been out of work for six months. She told me she was in the running for a wonderful part in a new movie. There were also three other excellent actresses being considered. After the auditions, she was sure the part was made for her, but she was not sure the producers would realize it.

"If I don't land this part," she said, "I don't know what I'll do. This could be a big step forward, or it could be the end of my career."

"You must be careful," I advised her. "The thought of competition engenders anxiety and tension, which clouds the working of the subconscious mind. In any case, it is always possible that you do not get cast, for reasons that have nothing to do with you or your abilities."

I went on to offer this suggestion. She should regularly declare, with faith and confidence:

> **I give thanks for my perfect expression at my highest level in Divine law and order. I accept my role in this film or something grander, greater, or more wonderful for me, according to the riches of the Infinite. It is God in action.**

Then I suggested she release the whole thing to her subconscious mind. Whenever the thought of the movie contract came to her, she was to tell herself, "Infinite Intelligence is taking care of that."

Mona was *not* cast for the part she had been so concerned about. Shortly afterwards, however, she received a wonderful offer, far more wonderful and exciting than the one she had desired originally. Her career has taken off, in a totally unexpected direction.

Whenever you are faced with what you believe to be competition for a job or assignment, persist in this simple procedure. Prepare yourself to receive an answer that will surprise and delight you.

The Marvelous Power of a Master Image

Your dominant or master image controls all phases of your life. Your subconscious accepts the dominant of two ideas. (For more on this, see *The Power of Your Subconscious Mind.**) Hugo B., a graphic designer for a software company in Los Angeles, visited with me for an hour about five years ago. He and his wife had two teenaged sons. His wife could not work because of severe allergies, made worse by the air pollution in Los Angeles. He earned a good salary, but it was not enough to support them adequately. They lived in a small bungalow in a rundown area and made do with only one car, a five-year-old economy model that was constantly breaking down.

I explained to Hugo how to use his imagination constructively. At my suggestion, he wrote down:

> I claim God's riches now, and my subconscious responds. I claim health, contentment, and a beautiful home for my family. My wife, my two boys, and I each need our own car, and my subconscious brings these requests to pass. Promotion is mine. Success is mine. I give thanks for the fulfillment of all this now.

Hugo and his wife made it a habit to mentally picture a spacious house and a lovely yard, in an area with clean air and friendly neighbors. They also pictured a garage with four cars. Before going to sleep each night, Hugo conveyed a message to his subconscious as follows:

> I am ever grateful for God's riches, forever active, forever present, unchanging and eternal. I give thanks for my promotion and outstanding success.

The Power of Your Subconscious Mind by Joseph Murphy, revised and expanded by Ian McMahan. Paramus, NJ: Reward Books, 2000.

For three months, nothing happened, but Hugo and his wife persevered with total confidence. Then, shortly after he was promoted to the head of his department, the company was bought out by a major software firm. Hugo's stock options were suddenly worth several million dollars. Moreover, the company's operations were transferred to Austin, Texas, where the air is clear, and he was able to buy a lovely, spacious home with a big yard for not much more than he received for the sale of his bungalow in Los Angeles. His wife's allergies have stopped bothering her, and their sons drive to their new high school in their own sporty little cars.

MEDITATION FOR EFFECTIVE IMAGINATION, THE WORKSHOP OF GOD FOR ALL GOOD

Where there is no vision, the people perish. (Proverbs 29:18) My vision is that I desire to know more of God and the way He works. My vision is for perfect health, harmony, and peace. My vision is the inner faith that Infinite Spirit leads and guides me now in all ways. I know and believe that the God-Power within me answers my prayer; this is a deep conviction within me.

I know that the mental picture to which I remain faithful will be developed in my subconscious mind and come forth on the screen of space.

I make it my daily practice to imagine for myself and others only that which is noble, wonderful, and God-like. I now imagine that I am doing the thing I long to do; I imagine that I now possess the things I long to possess; I imagine I am what I long to be. To make it real, I feel the reality of it; I know that it is so. Thank you, Father.

☞ CHAPTER POINTS TO REMEMBER ☞

1. The soul without imagination is what an observatory would be without a telescope. Imagination is the primal faculty of man, and it has the capacity to bring your idea into visibility on the screen of space.

2. You can draw up for yourself a treasure map listing the cherished desires of your heart. Go over it several times a day, claiming and imaging the fulfillment of each desire now. Persevere and you will find that the images will be deposited in the subconscious, which will bring them to pass.

3. If you are apprehensive and worried about the outcome of a conference or legal controversy, quiet your mind and claim that harmony, peace, and Divine understanding operate in the minds and hearts of all involved. Select the person who gave you the assignment and imagine she is telling you of the harmonious agreement and hear it over and over again. Lull yourself to sleep with the phrase, "happy ending." You will succeed in impregnating the solution in your subconscious, and there will be a Divine agreement.

4. A guide, strong in the conviction that he inherited the capacity of dowsing, convinced his subconscious mind that whenever he walked over an area where water was, his arm would become rigid and the wire in his hands would point to the exact spot. His subconscious responded to his conviction with successful divinations.

5. If you have trouble selling a home, imagine you are holding the check for full payment in your hand prior to sleep. Give thanks for the check, feel its reality, the naturalness and wonder of it all, and imagine yourself at the teller's window depositing it. Give thanks to your Higher Self and you will find wonders happening as you pray.

6. When you are competing with others for a contract, assignment, or position, avoid anxiety and tension by affirming, "I accept this assignment or something far more wonderful according to the riches of the Infinite for me." If you do not get that particular position, something far

more wonderful will open up for you in the light of your Higher Self.

7. Even though your reason and senses deny the possibility of your attaining riches, promotion, and success, persist in your master image for success and financial independence. Your master image will sink down into your subconscious mind and come to pass. Whoever perseveres will be crowned.

8. Make full use of the meditation at the end of the chapter to help develop your greater use of imagination for a richer life in every way.

How the Law of Infinite Increase Multiplies Your Wealth

All people throughout the world seek to magnify their personal good. A Divine urge whispers to men and women everywhere to rise, transcend, grow, and expand. This inner voice says insistently, "Come on up higher. I have need of you."

You want friends, a better position, a more comfortable life. You want to have enough money to stop worrying about it. You want enticing food, attractive and comfortable clothing, a home that meets your every need, a fine automobile, and all the other good things of life. Chances are, you also want to travel the world and see for yourself the beauties of nature and the beauties created by humankind. Above all, you want to learn more about the riches-producing laws of your mind, which will enable you to tap the treasure house of infinity within you and experience the life more abundant.

It is in the nature of soil to magnify and multiply the seeds you deposit in it. Plant an acorn in the ground, and you can in time look forward to a forest. But *God gave the increase* (I Corinthians 3:6). In the same fashion, when you plant thoughts of riches, abundance, security, and right action in your mind and water them with faith and expectancy, riches and honors will be yours.

Increase means the multiplication of your goods along all lines, spiritually, mentally, emotionally, socially, and financially. Every thought is incipient action. When you begin to think of the riches within your subconscious mind and all around you, you will be amazed how riches will flow to you from all sides.

One August, I conducted a seminar on a luxurious cruise ship that visited ports in Canada and Alaska. In Victoria, Canada, 18 students of the laws of mind joined me on the ship. We discussed the wonders and wisdom of the subconscious for the entire afternoon. Several of the participants told me that reading and applying the principles set forth in *The Power of Your Subconscious Mind** had transformed their lives, giving them a far greater measure of wealth, happiness, peace of mind, and fullness of life.

How He Used the Law of Increase for Great Wealth

One man who took part in our discussion, Jeremy M., was in heavy construction. He later told me that for many years he prayed continuallly that God would prosper him. At the same time, he spent much of his time brooding over his lack of money and the frail condition of his business. When he went to visit members of his family, he came away preoccupied by their financial plight. For days afterwards he could talk of little but their poverty. In his mind he practically clothed them in rags. He could not understand why neither he nor his relatives ever seemed to get ahead.

The Power of Your Subconscious Mind by Joseph Murphy, revised and expanded by Ian McMahan. Paramus, NJ: Reward Books, 2000.

One day, Jeremy heard a talk by an expert in mind science. Afterwards, he asked for a consultation. He described his plight and his puzzlement. Why were his prayers for prosperity never answered? The counselor explained that every thought is creative. As long as he continued to dwell on his own poverty and limitation, or on those of others close to him, he would effectively neutralize his own prayer and go on impoverishing himself.

This came as a revelation to Jeremy. He worked on reversing the current of his thoughts. He declared his conviction that God was prospering him in every way and was doing the same for his relatives. He began to claim God's riches for every person he met. Soon his condition changed radically for the better. His business flourished more than he could have imagined. Today he has two private planes to help him oversee the farflung operations of his construction firm.

Jeremy succeeded because he learned a great fulfilling law: What you wish for another, you are wishing for yourself. Or as an old Indian saying puts it, "The ship that comes home to my brother comes home to me."

How a Professor Used the Law of Increase to Her Personal Benefit

One of those who joined me on the cruise was Amanda R., a scholar in the field of philology. She told me that she attributed her success in her career only partly to the time, energy, and enthusiasm she brought to her teaching and research.

"I made it a point from the start," she said, "to rejoice in the accomplishments of my colleagues. I saw us as a team, working together for the advancement of human knowledge. Anyone's success, then, was my success as well."

"And what were the results?" I asked. I knew what her answer would be.

"My colleagues prospered," she replied. "They manifested greatly the law of increase and the riches of the omnipresent Divine bounty. It was only later that I realized another result, however. By appreciating and being happy about the good fortune of those around me, I was at the same time setting in motion a process that brought good fortune to me as well."

Amanda was quite right in her understanding. Her thoughts of success for others entered into her subconscious mind. Whatever is deposited in the subconscious may come forth magnified sixtyfold, a hundredfold, even a thousandfold. The result depends on the enthusiasm, the joy, and the intensity of the thought pattern. Today Amanda is one of the youngest full professors at an ancient and celebrated university. Rejoice in the idea of riches and ample supply for everyone, and you are certain to experience the law of increase in your own life.

How He Made a Dollar Increase into Important Wealth for Himself

In Juneau, Alaska, I got into a conversation with the man at the next table to me at lunch. When I admired his well-worn leather flying jacket, he said, "There's a story to that. I was given this jacket by my uncle, who was a fighter pilot when he was young. At one point I went through a pretty bad patch in my life. I wound up here in Juneau with just the clothes on my back and one single dollar bill in my pocket."

"Not a very comfortable situation," I remarked. "What did you do?"

"I found myself thinking about the fact that the whole world, and everything in it, comes from the mind of God," he replied. "I started walking, with the dollar folded up in my hand and a sentence going through my head, over and over.

'God multiplies this exceedingly, for it is God who giveth the increase.'"

He paused for a moment, shook his head, and continued. "I walked clear out of town. Suddenly I felt really hungry. I looked around and saw I was near the airfield. I went inside the terminal building and found a snack bar. When I asked the owner what I could get for a dollar, he said I could have whatever I wanted if I'd give him a hand. His counterman had quit the week before, and he was running around like a crazy man trying to do everything himself. The long and the short of it is, I stayed on. Pretty soon I was running the snack bar myself, with a share of the profits."

"So your dollar really did get multiplied exceedingly," I observed. "But where does your jacket come into it?"

"That's the really interesting part," he said. "One day as I was leaving work, a bush pilot who operated out of Juneau noticed my flight jacket. We got to talking, and the more we talked, the more I realized that I'd always wanted to fly, like my uncle. I started taking lessons, got my license and . . . well, seven years later, I own my own little fleet of charter planes. We fly people all over Alaska. It took a lot of hard work, but something else, too. I never could have succeeded if I hadn't looked to the Source of all blessings. I know that God's riches flow freely, joyously, and endlessly into my life."

Perpetual Opportunity for Increase Exists for You

Like the pilot I met in Juneau, you can use the laws of your mind to advance, move forward, and expand in every way. Give your best where you are working now. Be considerate, affable, amiable, loving, kind, and full of goodwill to all those around you and to all people everywhere. At the same time, don't be afraid to think big. Contemplate the law of opulence and growth, whose evidence you can see all around you. Bless what you are doing now, while realizing that it is simply a stepping-stone to your triumph and achievement. Recognize your true worth and claim wealth, promotion, and recognition in your mind. Be sure to claim riches and expansion for every person you meet during the day, whether it be your boss, your associate, your customer, or a friend. Make a habit of this, and you will succeed in impregnating your subconscious. Others will feel your radiation of riches and promotion, and the law of attraction will open up new doors of opportunity for you.

Why the Law of Increase Did Not Work for Him

"Your theories sound good," a man named Roger P. told me after a lecture. "But they don't work in practice. I've been affirming prosperity, abundance, and success twice a day ever since I first heard you speak last month, but I'm not getting anywhere. It's no wonder I'm in such bad shape. Every penny my business makes goes out again in taxes. I'm being eaten alive by a bunch of bureaucrats and welfare bums."

As we talked, I saw that, without realizing it, Roger was actually boasting about his financial difficulties. He blamed the government, taxes, unions, welfare, and the whole political system. His dearest belief was that he was a helpless victim of circumstance.

"Do you recall," I asked, "when I said that what you give your attention to, your subconscious mind absorbs and multiplies in your experience?"

"Of course I do," he replied, a bit impatiently. "Why do you think I spend the time affirming prosperity and so on?"

"How much time do you spend that way?" I asked.

"Why, five minutes every morning and evening," he said. "That's what you advise, isn't it?"

"And how much time do you spend every day thinking and talking about your financial problems, taxes, the government, and so forth?"

His face changed. "Oh, I see what you're getting at."

"As long as you continue to complain and harp on your financial troubles," I continued, "you will magnify them and impoverish yourself. As long as you see yourself as a victim, your subconscious mind will arrange for you to be victimized. As long as you blame outside factors for your problems, you will be prey to those factors. But when you begin to understand that you are master of the situation, you will *become* master of it. Those are the real laws of the mind."

How He Reversed His Faulty Thinking

At my suggestion, Roger reversed his thinking process. He began to see that he could begin to practice a creative process that would transcend circumstances and environmental conditions. His daily prayer was as follows:

> My business is God's business, and God's business always prospers. I use God's riches wisely, judiciously, and constructively to bless myself and others. I know the law of increase is now working and I am open and receptive to God's wealth and bountiful increase. I am richly and abundantly supplied within and without from the infinite storehouse of riches in my subconscious mind. By day and by night I am attracting more and more people who want what I have to offer. They are prospered and I am prospered. My mind and heart are open to the influx of God's riches now and forevermore.

As he fed his mind with these inner truths, Roger's business prospered and his outer supply became more abundant. At the end of a month, he noticed a tremendous change in his financial picture. He saw the great advantage in affirming the good and in ceasing to carp against lack and limitation. He discovered that attention to God's riches is the key to financial success.

The Significance of the Statement "My Cup Runneth Over" in the 23rd Psalm

During a recent tour of Europe, I paid a visit to the celebrated shrine of Fatima. While I was having lunch, a girl of about 16 came over to my table and said she had recognized me from my television broadcasts.

"I'm Gloria G.," she said, "from Anniston, Alabama, and I want to thank you for the letter and prayer you sent me last year. I did just what you said, and here I am."

"I'm glad to hear that, Gloria," I replied. "But I have to admit I don't recall writing you. Will you refresh my memory?"

"Oh, sure," she said. Her cheeks turned a little pink with embarrassment. "I wrote you to say that I really, really wanted to go to the Shrine of Fatima, but I didn't have the money. My parents knew how much I wanted it, and they approved. They would have helped if they could, but there's never anything left over at the end of the month."

"So I sent you a prayer," I said.

"That's right," she replied. She reached into her shoulder bag. "I'll show you. I always carry it with me."

She brought out a clear plastic case. Inside was a card with these words, carefully lettered by hand:

> **God opens up the way for me to go to the Shrine of Fatima during the summer in Divine order through Divine love.**

"I've been meditating on it first and last thing every day," Gloria explained. "And whenever I have a few moments during the day, too. And every night, before I go to sleep, I visualized the trip, taking the plane, landing in Portugal, going to the shrine . . . I tried to see and hear everything I would see and hear when I actually got here."

"Well," I said with a smile, "I can see that you did get here, so it must have worked."

"It sure did," she said emphatically. "What happened was, I spent a weekend with my friend, Jennifer. Her mom and dad said they were planning a vacation to Spain and Portugal, and I'm like, you've *got* to go to Fatima while you're there. I told them all about it, and they ended up inviting me to come along to keep Jen company."

The Bible says: *I go to prepare a place for you. And if I go and prepare a place for you, I will come again and receive you unto myself; that where I am, there ye may be also.* (John 14:2,3)

Gloria prepared the place she wanted to go in her disciplined imagination. She succeeded in impregnating her subconscious with the picture. Then her subconscious took over and acted on the minds of her friend's parents. They became the channel for the answer to her prayer.

Before she returned to her friends, Gloria shook my hand and said, "I really know now what it means when the Bible says, *My cup runneth over* (Psalm 23:5)."

"I'm sure you do," I replied. "And remember, it is written: *Ask, and it shall be given you* (Matthew 7:7)."

MEDITATION FOR YOUR BUSINESS OR PROFESSIONAL SUCCESS

Use the following powerful meditation to fill your cup of success in all things:

> I now dwell on the Omnipresence and Omniaction of God. I know that this Infinite Wisdom guides the planets on their courses. I know this same Divine intelligence governs and directs all my affairs. I claim and believe Divine understanding is mine at all times. I know that all my activities are controlled by this indwelling Presence. All my motives are God-like and true. God's wisdom, truth and beauty are being expressed by me at all times. The All-Knowing One within me knows what to do, and how to do it. My business or profession is completely controlled, governed, and directed by the love of God. Divine guidance is mine. I know God's answer, for my mind is at peace. I rest in the Everlasting Arms.

◠ CHAPTER POINTS TO REMEMBER ◠

1. All people throughout the world seek increase; it is the Divine urge within us seeking fuller, greater, grander expression in all phases of our lives. You plant wheat, barley, or oats in the soil, but it is God who giveth the increase by multiplying the grains a thousandfold.

2. Increase means the multiplication of your good along all levels.

3. Do not talk about the financial lack, poverty or sickness of others. To do so is to attract more lack to yourself. Clothe everybody mentally with the riches of God. Stop brooding about your own financial troubles and stop talking about your lack of money. Give attention to the riches of the Infinite within and without, and you will prosper. Attention is the key to life.

4. Rejoice in the advancement, good fortune, riches, and promotion of all those around you. Be exceedingly glad to see people experience, portray, and demonstrate the riches of God. As you do, you will attract riches of all kinds to yourself. Your thought is creative, and what you think about the other, you are creating in your own experience.

5. Be friendly with money, whether a dollar bill or a coin. Realize everything comes out of the invisible mind of God or of humans. Realize that God, or Infinite Spirit, is the Source of all blessings and that it is the nature of the Infinite to respond when you call upon it.

6. Give the best where you are working and the best will come back to you. Be friendly, affable, and amiable. Express goodwill to all. As you do, all doors will open up for your growth, expansion, and riches.

7. Form a clear mental picture of what you want to be, to do, or to have. Know that the power and the wisdom of

your subconscious will back you up. Persevere and be determined to become what you want to be. Your mental picture will be developed in your subconscious mind and become objectified.

8. When you are praying for increase in money, be sure to stop blaming the government, the welfare system, and taxes. To do so will cause money to fly from you rather than to you. What you want is more money. Realize that God's wealth is circulating in your life and that there is always a Divine surplus. What you criticize and condemn becomes manifest in your life. You become what you contemplate. Contemplate that God multiplies your good exceedingly, that your business is God's business, and that you are prospering beyond your fondest dreams.

9. If there is a journey you deeply long to make but cannot afford, affirm knowingly and feelingly, "God opens up the way for me to go on this journey in Divine order and through Divine love." Picture yourself boarding the plane and arriving at your destination. Enter into it in your imagination until you feel the tones of reality. Once you fix the picture in your subconscious, the way will open up, the dawn will appear, and all the shadows will flee away. *Ask, and it shall be given you* (Matthew 7:7).

10. The meditation at the end of the chapter will be of exceptional benefit to you in filling your cup of successful living.

10

How to Open the Gateway to Automatic Riches and Walk into a Life of Luxury

The gateway to infinite riches is hidden in that magic spiritual gem given to you in the Bible: *I am come that they might have life, and that they might have it more abundantly* (John 10:10).

Down through the ages, people have sought the key to riches and success, not knowing that the key was within themselves.

You are here to lead a full and happy life, to give expression to your hidden talents and release the imprisoned splendor within you. God is the giver and the gift, and all the riches of God are awaiting your discovery, application, and enjoyment.

By applying the laws of your mind, you can draw forth from the treasure house within you everything you need in order to lead a rich, glorious, and abundant life.

How She Opened the Gateway to Riches for Herself

A few years ago, I gave a class on Mental and Spiritual Laws in the Light of Emerson. One of those present was a young woman named Carol W., who had spent that morning going through the process of applying for workfare. She had two small children, and their father had recently walked out and disappeared.

I noticed her intent attitude as I quoted from Emerson and elaborated in light of the laws of mind. In one passage that particularly struck her—a favorite of mine, by the way— Emerson declares:

> In all my lectures, I have taught one doctrine—the infinitude of the private man, the ever-availability to every man of the Divine presence within his own mind, from which presence he draws, at his need, inexhaustible power.

Carol spoke with me afterwards and said that she remembered reading Emerson in college, but at that point nothing made an impression on her. The professor taught Emerson as a literary figure from nineteenth-century America, not as a great thinker with vital lessons for all of us today. Now, however, she saw him and his ideas in a totally new light. She announced that she intended to start using those ideas to draw from the Divine presence within her and promised to let me know the results.

How She Demonstrated Money

A few weeks later, Carol dropped by my office. Her face was transformed, like someone for whom great things had been done.

"My life is totally changed," she announced. "I want to tell you all about it, and I hope you will share my experience with others."

"I promise," I replied. "What have you done, and what are the results?"

"After your lecture," she said, "I went home and wrote a statement, a message I wanted to give to my subconscious mind. Here it is."

She passed me a card. On it was written,

I acknowledge and praise the Source within and I make contact with my thought. I give thanks that the gateway to riches is now open wide for me. God's riches flow freely to me, and more and more money is circulating in my life every day. Every day of my life I grow richer spiritually, mentally, financially, and in all ways. Money is God's idea circulating in my life, and there is always a surplus. I give thanks to *the living God, who giveth us richly all things to enjoy* (I Timothy 6:17).

"Several times a day," she continued, "I read this and declare it with feeling and enthusiasm. I realize now that as I shape my inner thought-life, my exterior life will follow. And it works!"

"Well, you know," I remarked, "Emerson said, 'The key to every man is his thought.' And it sounds as if you have discovered how to turn that key. Has it brought you the peace and prosperity you wish for?"

"And how!" she said with a smile. "right from the start, I found I was a lot calmer and more confident. I didn't yell at the kids, I didn't feel my heart sink every time I opened the mailbox and saw another stack of bills. I *knew* that the gateway was opening. Then yesterday, there was a letter in the box from a lawyer in Houston. When my grandfather passed on a couple of years ago, he left me and my cousins some mineral rights in West Texas. An oil company was leasing the exploration rights, but it was no big deal. My share came to about $50 a year. Now, though, they've made a big strike of natural gas. My royalties this year will be almost $100,000, and there could be even more in the future. Money *is* God's idea circulating in my life."

All Carol's financial troubles were over. She discovered that the gateway to prosperity was through her own subconscious mind. Its ways are past finding out.

How He Found the Gateway to True Expression

A while ago, I had a conversation with Timothy W., who had just been fired by the new director of the nonprofit organization where he had worked for 30 years.

"I'm at the end of my tether," he told me. "Everywhere I look, I've been turned down. They never say so, of course, but I know it's because of my age. If they give any reason—mostly they don't—they say things like needing fresh ideas and new approaches. I know what that really means. It means I'm not 25 anymore."

"Of course not," I said. "But your age is not what you're offering an employer. You are renting them your knowledge, experience, and wisdom that you have garnered through the years. What you are seeking is also seeking you."

At my suggestion, Timothy tried a new approach. Each night and morning he prayed, knowing that his subconscious mind was the gateway to expression, abundance, and the riches of life. This was his prayer:

> **Infinite Intelligence knows my hidden talents and opens up a new door of expression for me in Divine order. This knowledge is immediately revealed to my conscious mind. I will follow the lead that comes clearly and definitely into my mind.**

At the end of a week, he noticed a fund-raising ad on TV. He found a whole series of ideas come into his mind for modifying and sharpening the approach the group was taking. When he looked at the group's Website, he saw that one of their officers was someone he had met at a seminar a couple of years before. He made an appointment, went in, and explained his ideas. The officer listened, then said, "Tim, there is a place here for you if you can see your way clear to accepting it. We really need fresh ideas like yours."

Timothy accepted the offer at once. His salary and responsibilities proved to be far greater than in his previous position.

Remember, it is from within, not from without, that you get in touch with the riches of life. The electromagnetic waves that carry radio and TV programs permeate your environment, but if you want to benefit from a program, *you* must use the proper equipment and connect to the right frequency. It is the same with the wealth of the universe. It is all around us, but you must use the right equipment—your subconscious mind—and enter the right frequency—effective prayer—to get the results you want.

How a Trip to Japan Became a Reality

Tatsuko Y. is a young woman of Japanese origin who listens regularly to my morning radio program. In a letter, she told how the show had changed her life.

> I have dreamed of going to Japan to visit my grandmother, who is in her eighties, but the flight was much too expensive. One day I heard you say what to do if you want to take a trip and do not have a penny in your pocket. You said we should believe we had received the answer and to take some action to indicate our faith that our prayer was already answered in our deeper mind. I decided to try it. I made sure my passport was up to date, and I packed a suitcase with everything I would need and put it next to the door of my apartment.
>
> Next I spent time every morning and evening imagining my arrival in Japan, going to my grandmother's house, giving her a warm hug, and having a long talk in Japanese. I acted this out in my mind over and over, until it felt like something that was actually happening, not just an act of imagination.

Not long after I began this program, I ran into someone I knew from college. He told me he was just back from Australia. When I asked how he could afford such an expensive trip, he said he had gone as a courier. Companies sending delicate goods abroad often find it safer and faster to send them with someone as checked luggage. If you can go at short notice and restrict yourself to a carry-on bag, you can get amazing bargains.

I called a courier service that same afternoon. Two days later, they telephoned to ask me to escort some design mock-ups to Tokyo. They offered me a round-trip flight for $100! The next evening, I was embracing my grandmother just as I had imagined.

Please tell everyone to put their confidence in the strength of the Infinite within. Your good can come forth to you in unforeseen ways.

A Physicist Says Substance Is the Gateway to All the Money You Need

Ravi B. is a young physicist born in Madras, India, who visited me recently. He told me that his understanding of reality, shared by many modern physicists, is that Spirit and matter are one. Energy and matter are interconvertible and interchangeable. Matter is the lowest degree of Spirit, and Spirit is the highest degree of matter. In other words, they are both aspects of one and the same thing. Properly understood, matter is universal substance, or Spirit or Energy reduced to the point of visibility. The formed and unformed world are made out of the one substance we call Spirit. All things are made by the self-contemplation of Spirit.

Ravi told me, "I came to America on a very small fellowship, not nearly enough to survive, but I didn't get panicky. I knew the invisible would become visible. I declared in my heart, 'Divine Spirit is my instant and everlasting supply. It takes the form of food, clothing, money, friends, and everything I need right here and right now. I decree this and I know the manifestation takes place now, for God is the Eternal Now!'"

His declaration became manifest by way of a total stranger. They met in an elevator when the stranger remarked that he had recently returned from a business trip to India. He turned out to be head of the research arm of a major Silicon Valley chipmaker. When he heard what Ravi's specialty was, he immediately offered him a position in his lab, with a handsome salary and stock options.

Never underestimate the powers of personally affirming God, or the Living Spirit Almighty, your instant and everlasting supply that never fails. It will then manifest in countless ways and through many channels; perhaps through total strangers. Remember, you were born to be rich and inevitably to prosper along all lines through the use of your God-given faculties, which lie stretched in smiling repose within you.

How to Help Others to the Gateway to Riches, True Place, and Honor

When you wish to help a friend, a relative, an associate, or anyone who seeks your help to find his or her true place in life and become rich in livingness and givingness, use the following prayerful meditation in activating the forces for them:

> Infinite Spirit in its wisdom opens up the gateway for [*name*]'s true expression in life, where he [she] is doing what he [she] loves to do, is Divinely happy and Divinely prospered. He [she] is Divinely led to the right people, who appreciate his [her] talents, and he [she] receives marvelous and wonderful income for wonderful service. He [she] is conscious of

his [her] true worth, and he [she] is blessed and prospered
with God's riches beyond his [her] fondest dreams. I turn this
prayer over to my subconscious mind, which has the ability to
accomplish it. It brings it to pass in Divine order.

Repeat this prayer slowly, quietly, feelingly, and knowingly, pouring life, love, and enthusiasm into your words. You
will be amazed how the wisdom of the subconscious will respond. It never fails.

His Attitude Closed the Gateway to His Riches

Recently, during a lecture series in San Diego, a man came to
see me at my hotel. He introduced himself as Cliff A., a broker with a financial service, then said, "I've been praying
morning and night for prosperity and promotion, but it simply
doesn't work. I've got a good education, lots of experience,
everything it takes, but I'm not getting anywhere. Not only
that, I'm in a real bind financially. I've been trading heavily in
biotech stocks, on margin, and if something doesn't turn
around very soon, I'm going to end up wiped out. It's not my
fault, the people I talk to give me terrible advice. I think
maybe they have it in for me."

As we talked, I discovered that Cliff held many deep-
seated grudges and prejudices against his former employers as
well as his superiors at his current firm.

I explained to him that as long as his mind was cluttered
with hostility, grudges, and fears, his failure attitude would
neutralize all his prayers. It was a little like mixing an acid and
an alkali; one neutralized the other.

I suggested he redirect his mind, emphasize prosperous
thinking, and enter into the spirit of forgiveness for himself
and others. Accordingly, he began to meditate twice daily on
the following prayer:

I forgive myself for harboring negative and destructive thoughts, and I release my former employers and present associates to God completely, wishing for them all the blessings of life. Whenever I think of any one of them, I will immediately affirm, 'I have released you; God be with you.' I know as I continue to do this that I will meet them in my mind and that there will no longer be any sting present. I claim promotion now, success now, harmony now. Divine law and order are mine now. God's wealth flows to me in avalanches of abundance. Life is growth and expansion. I am an open channel for God's riches, which are ever-active, ever-present, unchanging, and eternal. I give thanks now for the riches within and without. What I am now decreeing comes to pass, and the light of God shines upon me.

Cliff followed this prayer process faithfully, taking care that he did not subsequently deny what he had affirmed earlier. He found himself attracting new people and being "led" to certain books, certain teachers, and certain classes on the subconscious mind. He discovered that he had set into operation subtle forces of his subconscious mind that correlated with his habitual thinking and prayer life. He was soon promoted to his firm's Los Angeles office with much higher pay. Moreover, one of the companies he had invested in received a patent on a valuable process. The stock tripled in a week. Cliff discovered that his changed attitude was really the gateway to fulfillment of his dreams. Dream noble and God-like dreams, and as you dream, so shall you become. You go where your vision is.

MEDITATION FOR OPENING THE GATEWAY TO RIGHT ACTION

The following meditation will establish judgment and confidence in taking the right action for any situation:

I radiate goodwill to all humankind in thought, word, and deed. I know the peace and goodwill that I radiate to every person comes back to me a thousandfold. Whatever I need to know comes to me from the God-Self within me. Infinite Intelligence is operating through me, revealing to me what I need to know. God in me knows the answer. The perfect answer is made known to me now. Infinite Intelligence and Divine wisdom make all decisions through me, and there is only right action and right expression taking place in my life. Every night I wrap myself in the mantle of God's love and fall asleep knowing Divine guidance is mine. When the dawn comes, I am filled with peace. I go forth into the new day full of faith, confidence, and trust. Thank you, Father.

☞ CHAPTER POINTS TO REMEMBER ☞

1. The gateway to infinite riches is based on the spiritual gem: *I am come that they might have life, and that they might have it more abundantly* (John 10:10). You are here to lead a full, happy, and rich life. You are here to squeeze the last drop of happiness out of life.

2. Emerson taught one doctrine—the infinitude of the private person. This means that the riches of the Infinite are within you. You can contact all the powers of the Godhead in you through your thought life. As you think of riches, guidance, inspiration, and creative ideas, there will be a response according to the nature of your thought. It responds by corresponding.

3. You are not selling your age to employers but your talents, abilities, wisdom, and experience garnered through the years. Realize that what you are seeking is also seeking you. Claim that Infinite Spirit is opening up a new door of expression for you where you are amply rewarded financially, and it will respond accordingly. It never fails.

4. If you want to take a trip anywhere around the world, act as though your prayer were answered. Do all the things you would do to prepare for the trip as if you actually

had the money in your pocket. Believe you have it now and you will receive it. In your imagination, feel yourself in that country or city now. Repeat the drama frequently until it gets into your subconscious, and then it will come to pass.

5. Spirit and matter are one. Energy and matter are one. The scientist uses the term energy for Spirit, which is God. God is the only presence, power, cause, and substance; therefore, Spirit is the reality of money, food, and clothing. The whole world of matter is simply Spirit in form, reduced to the point of visibility. Claim that God or Spirit is your instant and everlasting supply and that money is now flowing to you freely, joyously, and endlessly this very moment. Believe and know, realize and understand that the formless is forever taking form. Let money and all kinds of riches flow to you now.

6. When you wish to pray for riches and true expression for another, realize that Infinite Spirit opens up the gateway for his true expression and that God's riches are flowing to him in avalanches of abundance.

7. Changed attitudes change everything. If a person places emphasis on the spirit of forgiveness and goodwill to all and also forgives himself for harboring thoughts of failure, lack, and resentment, and then pours life, love, energy, and vitality into his thoughts of promotion, riches, expansion, honor, prestige, and recognition, his deeper mind will respond with compound interest, and his desert will rejoice and blossom as the rose.

8. Allow the meditation at the end of the chapter to penetrate your thinking for deciding on the right action to take.

How to Choose Your Wealth Goals and Receive Them Right Away

The Bible gives us the answer: *Choose you this day whom ye will serve* (Joshua 24:15).

The key to your health, wealth, prosperity, and success in life lies in your wonderful capacity to make decisions. The greatest discovery you can make is to awaken to the great truth that there is an infinite wisdom and power already established within you. It can enable you to solve all your problems and become wealthy, happy, joyous, and free. You were born to win. You are equipped with all the powers of God within you to make you master of your fate and captain of your destiny.

If you are not aware of your capacity to choose from the Kingdom of Heaven within you, which is the presence of God lodged in your deeper mind, you will instead choose and make decisions based on events, circumstances, and conditions around you. What is worse, in overlooking the powers within you, you will exalt the powers of circumstance that may exist at a certain time. Choose from the Kingdom of God within you and move forward on the high road to happiness, health, freedom, and the joy of living the abundant life.

The Power of Choice

Your power to choose is your most distinctive quality and your highest prerogative. Your capacity to choose and to initiate what is chosen reveals your power to create as a child of God.

How Her Power to Choose Transformed Her Life

"I don't know if I'm an alcoholic," Veronica V. told me, shame-facedly. "I do know I'm a compulsive drinker. It's more than I can handle, and it's ruining my personal and professional life. My whole future is in question."

"You say it's more than you can handle," I replied sympathetically. "I know how terrible that feels. But, in fact, you do have a mighty weapon in your struggle with this habit. You have the God-given capacity to choose . . . to choose sobriety, peace of mind, happiness, and prosperity, right here and right now."

"Tell me how," she replied. "I'll do anything to be free of this curse."

In response, I gave her the following prayer:

> I choose health, peace of mind, freedom, and sobriety right now. This is my decision. I know that the Almighty Power backs up my choice. I am relaxed, and God's river of peace flows through me. My spiritual food and drink are God's ideas and eternal verities, which unfold within me bringing me harmony, health, peace, and joy. In my imagination I am with my family, doing what I love to do. I am Divinely happy. Whenever the urge to drink comes, I remember these Divinely inspired ideas in my mind and the God Power backs me up.

Veronica repeated this prayer four or five times a day. She understood that she was writing these thoughts in her subconscious mind, which accepts repeated thought patterns affirmed convincingly and decisively. The shakes and the jitters still came occasionally, but each time she flashed on the screen of her mind the declaration she had made. Her desire to give up the bad habit was greater than her need to continue it, and the power of her subconscious backed her up.

The Riches of the Right Choice for Everyone

Every morning when you awaken, before you allow the concerns of the day to flood in on you, choose to recall and declare the following eternal truths. Remember that your lifetime experiences, conditions, and circumstances are the sum total of your choices. Affirm boldly as follows:

> Today is God's day. I choose harmony, peace, perfect health, Divine law and order, Divine love, beauty, abundance, security, and inspiration from On High. I know that as I claim these truths in my life, I awaken and activate the powers of my subconscious, which compel me to express all these powers and qualities. I know it is as easy for God to become all these things in my life as it is for a seed to become a blade of grass. I give thanks that this is so.

Every one of us, whatever our circumstances or calling, should make this choice every day. These are the principles of life. As you affirm them, you make all these powers of God active and potent in your life. Your subconscious accepts what you consciously believe, and it is easy for you to believe in the principles of harmony, peace, beauty, love, joy, and abundance.

Emerson said, "Nothing can bring you peace but the triumph of principles." There is a principle of beauty, but none of ugliness; there is a principle of harmony, but none of discord; there is a principle of love, none of hatred; there is a principle of joy, none of sadness; there is a principle of opulence and abundance, none of deprivation and poverty; and there is a principle of right action, none of wrong action. Begin to choose what is true of God and His goodness and the riches of life will be yours.

Decide to Choose the Riches of the Divinity Within You

Those who are afraid to make choices are actually refusing to recognize their own Divinity, for God indwells all people. It is your Divine right to make choices based on eternal verities and the great principles of life, which never change. Choose to be healthy, happy, prosperous, and successful, because you have dominion over your world of finance, business, health, profession, and relationships with others. Your subconscious mind is subject to the decrees and convictions of your conscious mind, and whatever you decree convincingly shall come to pass.

The Bible says: *Whatsoever a man soweth, that shall he also reap* (Galatians 6:7).

What Happens on Failing to Choose?

"I don't know what to choose," Greta M. told me. "How can I possibly tell what is reasonable or logical?"

"You *have* made a choice," I replied. "By deciding not to choose for yourself, you have chosen to accept whatever comes from the mass mind or the law of averages, in which we are all immersed. Suppose you go on vacation to a seaside resort. If you choose your room, you will have the view and facilities you want. If you do not choose your room, you will have whatever the desk clerk decides you should have. Do you trust the desk clerk more than yourself?"

"That wouldn't be very smart, would it?" she said thoughtfully. "If I really have the power to choose, it would be foolish not to choose thoughts, images, and ideals for myself.

Either I think for myself, or I let others do the thinking for me, in which case I'm stuck with whatever they decide."

By the end of our talk, Greta had decided to reverse her attitude. She began by asserting constructively:

> I am a choosing, volitional being. I have the power, the ability, and the wisdom to control and to direct my own mental and spiritual processes. I say to myself every morning when I awaken: God indwells me. What am I going to choose today from the treasure house of infinity within me? I choose peace, Divine guidance, and right action in my life. I decree that *Goodness, truth and mercy shall follow me all the days of my life: and I will dwell in the house of the Lord forever* (Psalm 23:6).

Following this manner of choice, Greta has transformed her life. Her health is better, she is more successful in her work, and her friends find her a loyal and sensitive companion.

The Infinite Power Backs Up Your Choices

You are a self-conscious individual. You have the capacity to choose. After deliberation, you select one jacket or pair of shoes in preference to another. You select your minister, doctor, dentist, home, wife or husband, food, and car. You are constantly being called upon to choose in this life. What kind of thoughts and images are you choosing? I want to reiterate and emphasize again that your whole life represents the sum total of your choices. Choose wisely, judiciously, and constructively. Choose the truths of God, which never change. They are the same yesterday, today, and forever.

Some say, "I will let God choose for me." When you say that, you mean a god outside yourself. God, or the Living Spirit, is omnipresent and is also within you, the very life of you. The only way God, or Infinite Intelligence, will work *for* you is to work *through* you. In order for the Universal to act on the individual plane, it must become the individual.

You are here to choose. You have volition and initiative. This is why you are an individual. Accept your Divinity and your responsibility and choose for yourself. Make your own decisions; some other person cannot possibly know what is best for you. When you refuse to choose for yourself, you are actually rejecting your Divinity and your Divine prerogatives. You are choosing to think from the standpoint of a slave, a serf, or an underling.

The Courage to Choose Transformed and Enriched Her Life

Thelma W. was a 54-year-old widow who ran a successful real estate agency in Santa Cruz, California. She came to me perplexed, baffled, and frustrated.

"I want to remarry," she told me. "The problem is, I've been seeing two different men. I'm fond of both of them, and they are both fond of me. They've both said things to indicate that marriage is on their minds too. But I can't marry them both, and I don't know how to make up my mind. Meanwhile, time is racing by. What do I do?"

"You've heard the story about the donkey, haven't you?" I replied. "It was halfway between two stacks of hay and it starved to death because it couldn't choose which one to eat from."

She laughed. "It's not really funny," she said. "That's just the way *I* feel!"

"You say you don't know how to make up your mind," I said. "That may be because you are trying too hard to force your conscious mind to choose. You have the ability to choose Infinite Intelligence within yourself to lead and guide you. Its nature was responsiveness. If you ask clearly and confidently, the answer will come to you."

"How will I know when it comes?" she worried.

"You'll know," I assured her. "It will be in a form that is impossible for you to miss."

That night, on going to sleep, Thelma spoke to her higher self as follows:

> **Father, you are all-wise. Reveal to me the answer and show me the way I should go. I give thanks for the right answer, for I know You know the only answer.**

During the night she had a dream that she remembered vividly the next morning. First one, then the other, of the men she was trying to choose between appeared to her. Each took her hand while she said a sad but definite "good-bye," then receded out of sight as if on an invisible conveyor belt. For a moment she stood alone in a featureless plain. Suddenly, a third man appeared. She recognized him at once. He was her late husband's best friend, who lived in the Midwest. She hadn't seen him in several years, but they had always gotten along very well. Just as he reached out both hands to her, the dream faded. She awoke feeling both desolate and oddly hopeful.

That very day, she received a card in the mail from the man. He had taken early retirement from his job with a power company and was strongly considering a move to Santa Cruz. He was coming later that week on a sort of scouting trip. Could she find time in her schedule to have dinner with him and show him around the town? She telephoned him the same day. Two months later, I had the pleasure of officiating at their wedding.

Thelma followed the biblical injunction, *Choose you this day whom ye will serve* (Joshua 24:15). If, like her, you turn to the Infinite Intelligence within you and call upon it, you, too, will receive the joy of the answered prayer. You can choose confidence, riches, and a full life. Many say that they have always experienced sickness, failure, frustration, and loneliness. All these failures can be dissolved by choosing to believe in the One Infinite Healing Presence. Feeling and emotion follow thought. You can, therefore, choose to build a new emotional life. Recognize that the will of God for you is the tendency of the Life-Principle itself, which seeks to flow through you as harmony, health, peace, joy, creative ideas, and prosperity, extending beyond your fondest dreams. You have chosen to believe that what is true of God is true of you. Therefore, from this moment forward the preponderance of your thought and expectancy will come from Him who giveth to all life, breath, and all things. Your mind and heart will be always open for the influx of God's riches now and forevermore.

MEDITATION FOR BUILDING YOUR ACCOUNT AT YOUR PROSPERITY BANK

I know that my good is this very moment. I believe in my heart that I can prophesy for myself harmony, health, peace, and joy. I enthrone the concept of peace, success, and prosperity in my mind now. I know and believe these seeds will grow and manifest themselves in my experience.

I am the gardener; as I sow, so shall I reap. I sow God-like thoughts of peace, success, harmony, and goodwill. The harvest is wonderful.

From this moment forward I sow in my subconscious mind thoughts of peace, confidence, poise, and balance. I harvest the fruit of the wonderful seeds I sow. I believe and accept the fact that my desire is a seed deposited in the subconscious. I make it real by feeling the reality of it. I accept the reality of my desire in the same manner I accept the fact that the seed deposited in the ground will grow. I know it grows in the darkness; also, my desire or ideal grows in the darkness of my subconscious mind. In a little while, like the seed, it appears above the ground as a condition, circumstance, or event.

Infinite Intelligence governs and guides me in all ways. I meditate on whatsoever things are true, honest, just, lovely, and of good report. I think on these things, and God's power is with my thoughts of good. I am at peace.

⌒ CHAPTER POINTS TO REMEMBER ⌒

1. The key to your health, wealth, prosperity, and success lies in your capacity to choose. Choose whatsoever things are true, lovely, noble, and God-like. Choose thoughts, ideas, and images that heal, bless, inspire, dignify, and elevate your whole being.

2. Your power to choose is your highest prerogative, enabling you to select from the infinite treasure house within you all the blessings of life.

3. When an alcoholic chooses to select harmony, peace, sobriety, and right action in life, knowing the Almighty power will back up the choice, that person is on the way to release from her habit, and to freedom and perfect health. She uses the wonderful power of disciplined imagination in realizing that she is doing what she loves to do, dramatizing the liberating thought over and over again until it has all the tones of reality. The minute the idea of freedom is fixed in her subconscious mind, she is compelled to freedom and sobriety.

4. A wonderful choice for everyone every morning of life is to affirm: "Divine right action is mine. Divine law and order govern my life. Divine peace is mine. Divine love fills my soul. Divine harmony reigns supreme. Divine beauty fills my soul. I am inspired and Divinely led in all ways. There is a happy outcome to all my undertakings." Make a habit of this and wonders will happen in your life.

5. Never hesitate to make a choice. You are a volitional, choosing being, and to refuse to choose is actually to reject your own Divinity. You can choose according to universal truths and principles of God, which never change.

6. In failing to choose for yourself, you are actually saying that you are going to let the mass mind, full of irrational fears, superstitions, and ignorance of all kinds make

choices for you. If you do not choose to do your own thinking, the mass mind and the propaganda of the world will make choices for you. There is no such thing as indecision. It simply means you have decided not to decide. Don't let others make up your mind. Choose God and His truth.

7. Choose that goodness, truth, and beauty will follow you all the days of your life because you dwell in the house of God forever.

8. Your whole life consists of a series of choices. All of your experiences are the sum total of your choices. You are always choosing your books, clothes, schools, partners, homes, cars, and so on. Watch the kind of thoughts, images, and ideas you choose. You are what you think all day long. Choose what is lovely and of good report.

9. God, or Infinite Intelligence, will do nothing for you except through your thought, images, and choices. The Universal cannot act on the individual except it becomes the individual.

10. Choose God and realize that only God knows the answer. If perplexed and wondering how to choose between two alternatives, realize that God, or Infinite Intelligence, knows the answer. Contemplate the answer and the Supreme Intelligence will respond accordingly. It never fails.

11. Regardless of past errors, sickness, and failures, believe now the absolute truth that the will of God for you is a greater measure of life, love, truth, and beauty, transcending your fondest dreams. Open your mind and heart and live in the joyous expectancy of the life more abundant now and forevermore.

12. Use the meditation at the end of the chapter to build up your account in the prosperity bank.

How to Hear the Gentle, Invisible Voices That Can Guide You to Wealth

Your subconscious mind seeks to protect you at all times, so you should learn to listen to the inner promptings of intuition. Your subjective self governs all your vital organs. It will continue to maintain them in equilibrium and balance unless your conscious mind intrudes with worry, anxiety, fears, and negative thoughts. These negative thoughts upset the Divine norm within your deeper mind. Within your subconscious mind is the Divine presence, which some call the Higher-Self, the Superconscious, the I AM, or The Christ in you, the hope of Glory. All these terms mean the same thing.

Your subconscious mind reacts to suggestion and the commands of your conscious mind. Because of this, you can train your conscious mind to recognize the promptings of your subjective mind in the right direction. When you are relaxed and your mind is at peace, your conscious mind is more closely in rapport with your subconscious mind. Then the inner voice of intuition is heard and felt clearly and distinctly.

She Was Glad She Listened to That Inner Voice

Jean Wright, my secretary for many years, told me that some years ago she and her mother planned to go away for a weekend. On Saturday morning, however, she had that inner feeling, a deep-seated hunch, that seemed to say, "Don't go. Stay at home." She tried to brush it aside, but the feeling persisted. Finally she responded and stayed home.

Two hours later, while her son was playing at the beach nearby, he tripped and banged his face into a railing. One of his front teeth was knocked out. Because Jean was on hand, she was able to retrieve the tooth and get her son to a dental surgeon immediately. The dentist managed to implant the damaged tooth, and her son did not suffer any permanent damage. She later learned that the dental surgeon had been on the point of leaving on an overnight journey the moment she called. If she had been even five minutes later, her son would have lost the tooth. Her inner prompting was correct in every way.

How to Follow and Recognize the Voice of Intuition

When you need to decide on a course of action, the best guide you could possibly have is the knowledge that comes from giving your subconscious mind the correct instructions. This will enable you to distinguish the true from the false. When you have a sincere desire for the truth, knowing that Infinite Spirit responds according to the nature of your thought, you will get results.

Use the following prayer frequently:

> Infinite Intelligence is my constant guide and counselor. I will instantly recognize the promptings and monitions that come from my Higher-Self, which forever seek to protect,

guide, and watch over me in all ways. I will instantly recognize the lead which comes into my conscious mind, and I will always disregard groundless fancies. I know that my deeper mind responds to what I am now consciously writing on it, and I give thanks for the joy of the answered prayer.

As you form the habit of using this prayer regularly, you will become able to recognize instantly the interior voice by the inward sense of touch it gives you. This will make it possible for you to differentiate and distinguish between the false and the true.

How Cultivation of the Intuitive Faculty Brings Riches to You

On the basis of what you consciously meditate upon, you will receive answers and directions from your subconscious mind. The question you entertain or turn over to your deeper mind gestates in the darkness of your subconscious. When all the data are gathered, you receive instantaneously an analysis and conclusion that your intellect, or reasoning mind, might require weeks of monumental trial and error to accomplish. When our reasoning faculties fail us in our perplexities, the intuitive faculty sings the silent song of triumph.

Artists, poets, writers, and inventors listen to this voice of intuition. As a result, they are able to astonish the world by the beauties and glories drawn from this storehouse of knowledge within themselves. They have discovered the source of true riches.

The Infinite Riches of Intuition Saved His Life

Many of you may have read about a Japanese air disaster in which so many unfortunate people lost their lives. Some weeks later, I received a letter from a Japanese student. He wrote:

I have been reading your work, *The Power of Your Subconscious Mind*,* which has much impressed me. I was ticketed to go on the aircraft flight that ended so tragically. As I was about to leave for the aeroport, an inner voice spoke to me. It said quite clearly, "Do not go. Do not go." It was as clear as a message over a loudspeaker. Because of your book, I knew that I should listen. I did not go. I believe I have been saved so that I can tell others about the wonderful powers of the subconscious mind.

Intuition and What It Means

Intuition means the direct perception of truth, independent of any reasoning process. It is an immediate apprehension, a keen and quick insight. The word "intuition" also means "inner hearing." Hearing is not the only way to nurture intuition. Sometimes it comes as a thought, but the most common way is to "hear the voice." Intuition goes much farther than reason. You employ reason to carry out intuition. Very often you will find that intuition is the opposite of what your reasoning would have told you.

The conscious mind of man is reasoning, analytical, and inquisitive; the subjective faculty of intuition is always spontaneous. It comes as a beacon to the conscious intellect. Many times it speaks as a warning against a proposed trip or plan of action. We must listen and learn to heed this inner voice of wisdom. It does not always speak to you when you wish it to do so, but it will when you need it.

She Had a Persistent Feeling That She Should Not Accept the Position

"I'm in a real quandary," Louise B. told me. "I'm a little bored with my present job, so I registered with one of these new online headhunters. The next thing I know, I get a fabulous offer

---

The Power of Your Subconscious Mind by Joseph Murphy, revised and expanded by Ian McMahan. Paramus, NJ: Reward Books, 2000.

from a high-tech startup. More responsibility, a big boost in salary, stock options, travel . . . It's like a dream. My boyfriend tells me I'd be a total idiot if I didn't grab it."

"And . . . ?" I prompted.

"I can't," she said. "I don't know why. I know Greg must be right, and I'm sure I'll be sorry down the road, but something keeps telling me not to take it. Isn't that crazy?"

"Not at all," I said forcefully. "What you are hearing is probably the voice of your subconscious mind. It has ways of knowing that are beyond our conscious ken. You must decide for yourself what to do, but I urge you not to brush aside your intuitive feeling."

"That's what I hoped you'd say," she told me. Relief was painted plainly on her face. "I'm going to call them this afternoon and turn down the offer."

Three weeks later, I found a message from Louise on my voice mail. "My subconscious must be really on the ball," she said. "That company that wanted to hire me just went belly-up. Chapter Eleven. If I hadn't taken your advice and listened to my intuition, I'd be in a real mess now."

Louise's conscious mind (and her boyfriend) may have been right in terms of the facts that were objectively available and known, but her intuitive faculties understood other aspects of the situation. Before she permitted her objective mind to argue with her inner knowledge, she came to a quick decision that proved to be correct in every way. She later told me that, since that experience, she has made it a habit, after praying about anything, to follow the first impression that comes to her. She has found that it is always correct.

The Riches of Clairaudience

Clairaudience is a term that means "clear hearing." It is a faculty of your subconscious mind. A classical example is the demon that the great Greek philosopher Socrates described. He believed he could clearly hear this inner voice, whose admonitions were always wise. The voice was usually one of warning. Moreover, he pointed out that its strongest manifestations came when his safety or well-being was involved. His subconscious mind communicated with the conscious mind in words audible to his senses.

This phenomenon is based on the most powerful instinct of the human soul—the instinct of self-preservation. Socrates believed that the silence of the demon was an approval of his conduct, and according to his belief was it done unto him.

How the Voice of Intuition Proved to Be a Lifesaver

A young woman named Lorinda H. was invited to visit relatives in a distant city over a Labor Day weekend. Another guest could give her a ride. Even as she was talking to her cousin on the phone, Lorinda's inner voice spoke to her clearly. It told her, "Stay home! Stay home!" She followed the advice and turned down the invitation. She later found out that the young woman who was supposed to pick her up was killed in a multicar pileup on the freeway.

For several years, since beginning to attend our meetings and lectures, Lorinda has directed her subconscious mind to supply her with guidance. She lives in the certain knowledge that Divine right action will govern her. She constantly affirms that she will be instantaneously warned by the wisdom of her subconscious about anything she needs to know for her welfare and spiritual protection. It has never failed her. Through repetition she has conditioned her subconscious to respond, and the intelligence enables her conscious mind to receive communication from her subjective mind by means of spoken words. It is one way of bringing the wisdom of her deeper mind to her surface or objective mind. The sound she hears is subjective; it does not cause atmospheric vibrations; but its reality is clear to her nonetheless.

These sounds or mental stimuli are distinct to her but are not perceptible to others who may be near her. You can employ this technique with fabulous dividends in all phases of your life.

A Broker Discovers the Riches of Intuition

A broker friend of mine, Philo L., invests solely on his own account and those of a few wealthy clients. His special field of interest is small-cap stocks. Ordinarily, these are very speculative, but they offer rich rewards for those who are successful. Philo has had extraordinary success in this field. Some months ago, the name of such a stock welled up in his mind. His inner voice said, "Buy it." He did so and also put his clients into it. In the time since, he and his clients have realized profits of several hundred percent.

Philo's secret of success is that he trusts and listens to the voice of intuition. He makes a practice of charging his subconscious mind as follows:

> **My subconscious mind will make me instantly aware of the right stock to buy, at the right time, in the right way. This will bless me and my clients.**

It is obvious that Philo has succeeded in getting the intuitive faculty of his subconscious to respond according to the nature of his request. The magic of extrasensory perception is alert to his request and presents him with the information he needs at the right moment.

A Most Extraordinary Experience

An old friend, Fred W., admitted to me that at one time he had been on the verge of committing suicide. "I had just lost my wife and baby in an automobile accident," he said, with tears welling up at the memory. "I was sure that the world held nothing more for me except misery. I held a pistol to my temple. But just as I placed my finger on the trigger, I heard a voice. It was the most commanding voice I've ever heard. It said, very clearly, 'Not now! With long life will I content you!' I was stunned. The thought of going against such a command was unthinkable. I put the pistol down. Later I threw it in the river, in case the temptation to do away with myself returned."

"What an amazing experience," I commented. "When did this happen?"

"Oh, long before we met," he replied. "I was just in my twenties at the time. Since then, I've become convinced that I was spared for a reason. I never ignore the promptings of my inner voice."

What Fred learned from this searing experience is that when danger to the individual is imminent, the subjective mind makes a supreme effort to avoid and prevent the danger. It acts and speaks in a way to which the individual will respond. The highest activity of your subconscious, or subjective mind (I use these words interchangeably), is exercised in the effort to preserve the life of the individual.

Remember, the monitions of your deeper self are always lifeward and should be heeded. That inner voice that seeks to protect you physically, emotionally, spiritually, financially, and in all ways is not from supernatural agencies or disembodied entities but from the intuitive faculty of your own subconscious, which knows all and sees all.

A Remarkable Encounter in London

Some years ago, I lectured in England. My sister told me that a cousin of ours was living in London, a man I had gone to school with as a boy. She had no idea where he lived or what his occupation was, but a friend of hers had mentioned he was in London.

I checked the telephone book, but his name was not there. Instead of giving up the quest, I followed this procedure. I imagined myself meeting him, shaking hands with him, and talking over old times. I did this every night before I went to sleep. Finally, my week's stay in London came to an end. I was scheduled to leave for Switzerland in a few hours. I decided to send off some letters and postcards, and I remembered there was a post office around the corner from St. Ermin's Hotel, where I always stay in London. As I was waiting in line, I heard a familiar voice saying, "Well, Joe! Fancy meeting you here!"

Everything I had pictured and felt as true in my mind came true. We had time for a wonderfully moving and amusing reunion before I had to leave to catch my plane. The wisdom of my subconscious mind had brought both of us together in Divine order. The ways of the deeper levels of your mind are past finding out. Let the wonders and riches of intuition happen to you.

MEDITATION FOR THE RICHES OF THE SILENCE

Jesus said, "God is a Spirit; and they that worship him must worship him in spirit and in truth."

I know and realize that God is a spirit moving within me. I know that God is a feeling or deep conviction of harmony, health, and peace within me. It is the movement of my own heart. The spirit or feeling of confidence and of faith that now possesses me is the spirit of God and the action of God on the waters of my mind. This is God. This is the creative Power within me.

I live, move, and have my being in the faith and confidence that goodness, truth, and beauty shall follow me all the days of my life. This faith in God and all things good is omnipotent. It removes all barriers.

I now close the door of the senses; I withdraw all attention from the world. I turn within to the One, the Beautiful, and the

Good. Here, I dwell with my Father beyond time and space; here, I live, move, and dwell in the shadow of the Almighty. I am free from all fear, from the verdict of the world, and from the appearance of things. I now feel His Presence, which is the feeling of the answered prayer, the presence of my good.

I become that which I contemplate. I now feel that I am what I want to be. This feeling or awareness is the action of God in me. It is the creative Power. I give thanks for the joy of the answered prayer and I rest in the silent knowledge that "it is done."

☞ CHAPTER POINTS TO REMEMBER ☞

1. Your subconscious mind seeks to protect you at all times, and it behooves you to learn to listen to its inner monitions and promptings at all times.

2. When you are relaxed and your mind is at peace, the inner voice of intuition is heard clearly and distinctly.

3. The inner voice often speaks to you as an inner, persistent feeling, a sort of hunch warning you of danger to yourself or a loved one. A mother who followed her hunch was able to get prompt assistance for her son.

4. When you have a sincere desire for the truth and know that Infinite Spirit responds according to the nature of your thought, you will get results. Affirm boldly that Infinite Intelligence is your constant guide and counselor and that you will instantly recognize the monitions of your Higher-Self. You will receive answers according to your request.

5. You will receive answers and directions from your subconscious according to what you meditate on.

6. Artists, poets, inventors, and other creative people listen to the inner voice of intuition. They astonish the world

by the beauties and glories drawn from the storehouse within.

7. A Japanese student heard an inner voice saying clearly to him, "Don't go on the plane." He followed the instruction. Shortly thereafter, that particular plane was involved in a tragic air disaster. He has trained his subconscious mind to watch over him in all his ways.

8. Intuition means direct perception of truths or facts independent of any reasoning process. Intuition also means, "inner hearing."

9. The extrasensory faculties of your deeper mind can see the motivations of an employer and also the future result. These are hidden from the conscious mind. When that intuitive feeling wells up telling you not to take a new position, follow it.

10. After praying about anything specific, the first impression is usually correct.

11. Clairaudience is a faculty of your subconscious and means "clear hearing." Self-preservation is the most powerful instinct of the human soul. Many times your subjective self speaks in a voice to warn you and to protect you.

12. You can direct your subconscious to guide you always and know that Divine right action governs you. You will be instantly informed about anything you need to know for your protection. If you hear a voice saying, "Don't go!"—obey it.

13. A successful broker conveys the idea to his subconscious mind that he will be instantly made aware of the right stock to buy or sell. The names of particular stocks well up from his subconscious, and he becomes consciously

aware of the right course of action to follow for himself and his clients.

14. When danger to the individual is imminent, the subjective mind makes a supreme effort to avoid danger. It may speak in a way to which the individual will respond.

15. The monitions of your deeper mind are always lifeward and should be heeded.

16. If you wish to meet someone and you don't know where the person is, picture yourself talking to the individual, feel the reality of the experience, dramatize it in your mind, and enter into the tones of reality. Your deeper mind will bring both of you together in Divine order.

17. To avail yourself of the amazing riches of the silence, use the meditation at the end of the chapter.

13

How Your Money Dreams Can Make You Rich—The Secret of Psychic Osmosis

In his essay on self-reliance, the brilliant New England philosopher Ralph Waldo Emerson says: "Trust thyself: Every heart vibrates to that iron string. Accept the place the Divine providence has found for you, the society of your contemporaries, the connection of events. Great men have always done so and confided themselves childlike to the genius of their age, betraying their perception that the absolute trustworthy was seated at their heart, working through their hands, predominating in all their being."

What is Emerson telling us? That God indwells us, that the absolute trustworthy is seated in our hearts, and that all we have to do is to permit ourselves to vibrate or tune in on the Infinite within and receive all the blessings and riches of life. He is saying that you are Life, or God manifested, and that you are an instrument of Life's expression. You are unique. There is no one in all the world like you, because you are you. Your thumbprint, the rhythm of your heart, the pattern of your retina, the secretions of your glands, the information encoded in every cell of your body are different from those of any other person in the entire history of our species. Infinite differentiation is the law of life. Your thoughts, your attitudes toward life, your beliefs and convictions, all are your own and different from those of others.

You were born with your own particular endowments, talents, abilities, and special inherent gifts. You are here to express more and more of the God-Presence and to experience the joy of living the life more abundant. You are uniquely equipped to express life in a way and manner that no one else in all the world can do. You want to be what you want to be, you want to do what you love to do, and you want to have all the good things of life.

You can achieve all these goals in life because you are endowed with the qualities and faculties of imagination, thought, reason, and the power to choose and act. Let Life flow through you as harmony, beauty, love, joy, health, wealth, and fullness of expression.

How a Teacher Instills the Riches of Self-Confidence in His Pupils

Is it not written in your law, I said, Ye are gods? (John 10:34).

Hugo D. is a young man who teaches Sunday School in Las Vegas. He confided to me that many of the children he taught were shy, timid, and diffident. Some of them seemed to suffer from a profound inferiority complex.

"I saw it as a part of my duty toward them to show them a path toward a greater appreciation of their own value," he told me. "So I wrote an affirmation on the blackboard. I told them to copy it and repeat it for five minutes every night before going to sleep."

"How does it go?" I asked, intrigued by his personal discovery of this technique.

"This is what I gave them," he replied:

> I am a child of the Living God. God loves me and cares for me. I am different, and God wants to do something special through me. God watches over me and guides me, as I am

growing in strength, love, and wisdom. My Heavenly Father loves his child. He walks and talks in me.

He added, "I told them that as they used it and affirmed it every day, there would be a response from the God-Presence. They would grow in wisdom, strength, and power and would become outstanding students, successful in college, and rich in all the blessings of life."

"What were the results?" I asked.

"Since then, they have been practically blossoming," he said enthusiastically. "Their confidence and self-reliance has grown wonderfully. They are relating better to their parents, too. It's just amazing. I really believe that I am seeing God at work."

What Hugo did with this technique was to instill into the minds and hearts of these children the knowledge that God indwells them and that He would respond to the simple prayer of their hearts. They came to realize, as Emerson said, that the absolutely trustworthy was seated at their heart working through them at all times.

The True Meaning of Self-Confidence

Confidence means "with faith." Faith is a way of thinking, an attitude of mind, an understanding of the laws of mind. It is an awareness that your thought and feeling create your destiny. You have faith when you know that any idea felt as true by your conscious mind will be impressed on and accepted by your subconscious mind and be manifested on the screen of space. In simple, everyday language, your faith is an awareness of the presence and power of God (the Living Spirit Almighty) within you. Through your contact with this Presence and through the medium of your thought you can live a victorious and triumphant life. You will find yourself meeting all obstacles, difficulties, and challenges head on, realizing that they are all Divinely outmatched. Tuning in on the Divine presence within you, you can move through the vicissitudes of life with a deep abiding trust that you can do all things through the God-Power that strengthens you.

How She Developed Self-Confidence and Became Rich and Successful

Recently a young entrepreneur named Laurie Y. came to see me. In the few years since leaving college, she had started two Internet-related companies, both of which stirred some excitement, then eventually went under. Now she was down on herself, full of self-criticism.

"I think I'm fooling myself," she said. "And fooling everybody who's been trusting enough to invest their money in my ideas, too. I just don't have what it takes these days. I look around and see these kids, five or six years younger than me, and I realize I'm not on the cutting edge any more. I'm through!"

"What those kids have, you have as well," I told her. "Within you is Infinite Intelligence. It created the world and knows no obstacles. What is more, it can reveal to you everything you need to know. You are born to succeed and triumph in life, because Infinite Intelligence, or God, cannot fail. Nothing can oppose, challenge or vitiate the movement of omnipotence."

Her face brightened, but she still seemed doubtful.

"There is more," I continued. "As you gain confidence in the God-Self within you, you'll find that it is contagious. You will radiate assurance, faith, poise, and balance. You will become a spiritual and mental magnet, attracting good to yourself from all sides. Always recall one of the most powerful spiritual gems of truth in the Bible: *If God be for us, who can be against us?* (Romans 8:31)."

Here is the specific formula that worked wonders for Laurie. Every morning after brushing her teeth, she looked directly at her reflection in the mirror and said aloud, feelingly and knowingly: "If God be for me, who can be against me? I can do all things through the God-Power that strengthens me. Success is mine and riches are mine. Thank you, Father."

She repeated these great biblical truths for four or five minutes every morning, knowing that as she was sincere, these truths would penetrate by osmosis from her conscious mind to her subconscious. Because the law of the subconscious is compulsive, she would in this way be compelled to express success and riches.

A few weeks later, Laurie woke in the middle of the night with a brilliant new concept. She stayed up until dawn drafting an initial business plan. When she tried it out on a former partner, he said she must get in touch with a friend of his, Dan B., who was thinking along related lines. When she and Dan met, they discovered that they thought alike in many ways, not just in business. They became partners and raised venture capital to start a new company that is now planning to offer stock in the market. They are also talking seriously about a closer personal relationship.

Such experiences are commonplace today with men and women who begin to tap the tremendous potentials within them. There are many more millionaires and billionaires now in the United States than at any previous time in history.

Allow Yourself Success and the Riches of the Infinite

The Life-Principle, which some call God, is forever seeking to express itself at higher levels through you. There is an urge in you that constantly prompts you to rise higher and higher. This Presence and Power is all-wise. It knows all and sees all. It is omnipotent and supreme. Insist on the best in life; refuse the second best. Concentrate your thought, feeling, and attention on your profession, realizing that the Infinite Intelligence of your subconscious is constantly revealing to you new creative ideas and better ways in which to serve.

Realize that you are one with the Infinite and that the Infinite cannot fail. Emerson said, "No one can cheat you out of ultimate success but yourself." The English philosopher, Thomas Carlyle, said: "The wealth of a man is the number of things he loves and blesses which he is loved and blessed by." Or as the great poet Samuel Taylor Coleridge wrote:

> *He prayeth well who loveth well*
> *Both man and bird and beast.*
> *He prayeth best who loveth best*
> *All things both great and small;*
> *For the dear God who loveth us,*
> *He made and loveth all.*

It is not fate that blocks your success or riches, nor lack of money, introductions, or contacts. It is yourself. All you have to do is to change your thought-life and keep it changed. Let your habitual thinking be: "Success is mine, God's wealth is mine, harmony is mine, and I am a channel for all the riches of God." Your thoughts are creative; you become what you think all day long.

Millions of people claim to believe in a variety of creeds, dogmas, sects, traditions, amulets, charms, icons, shrines, and so on, but because they have no real workable faith, their lives are chaotic and confused. Millions suffer from lack and poor health and barely eke out a living, because they are unaware of how to tap the treasure of infinity in their own subconscious mind.

Millions of other people have a real workable faith. They demonstrate it daily in their bodies, their business, their finances, their human relations, and in all other phases of their lives. A person's faith in God must be personally demonstrated. It will show itself by the light in his eyes. Affluence is a sign of faith in the law of opulence. An attitude of trust and understanding of the bountiful nature of the providence of God is reflected in a person's confidence in himself and the powers within him. It is manifest in his positive manner, gestures, speech, and the sunshine of his smile.

A Lonely Bachelor Discovers the Riches of Self-Confidence

"I don't know why I can never meet anyone who clicks with me spiritually," Leo D. told me sadly. "Maybe I've worked so hard that I never had time to learn the right kind of social skills. Or maybe I'm simply a born loser."

"Losers are made, not born," I replied. "If you cling to thoughts of loss, of isolation, of being alone and unlovable, you *attract* those qualities to yourself, both within and without. However, once you begin to recognize your innate qualities, which are the sign of the Infinite within, you manifest those qualities on the screen of reality. That, in turn, draws to you those who are spiritually prepared to respond to them."

I gave Leo a simple technique to use. I told him to visualize himself in a beautiful and soul-enriching setting, such as a lovely beach or woodland glade. He was talking to someone whose qualities were as manifest as his own. Each of them acknowledged and honored the Infinite Intelligence and Goodness that joined them. He was to imagine this scene, in as much detail as possible, every morning on awakening and every night before going to sleep.

"Remain faithful to this picture in your mind," I told him. "You want to meet the ideal, spiritual-minded partner. Seeing yourself with that person means it has already happened in your mind. What has happened in your mind must take place objectively, irrespective of any seeming difficulties and obstacles that seem to stand between you and the realization of your mental image. You will triumph, and you will be happy, joyous, and free."

Leo took my advice. He formulated the image of the relationship he desired as if he had already achieved it and thanked the God-Presence within him for it. He did this each morning and night. At the end of about 10 days, he saw a brochure for a spiritual retreat at a seaside location. The photo of the beach exactly matched the spot he had imagined. He signed up for the retreat and while there, met a young woman whom he immediately recognized as the one in his visualization. I later had the pleasure of conducting the wedding ceremony for them.

Realize there is always an answer. There is Someone who cares—that One who created you loves you and watches over you at all times, asleep or awake.

A Real Estate Dealer Discovers the Riches of Self-Confidence

Deborah W. came up to me after a lecture and handed me her card.

"So you're in real estate," I observed. "How are things going for you?"

"Terrible," she replied. "Housing values have been rising so fast that most people are being priced out of the market. The rise in interest rates is killing us, too. There's no way I can make a decent living in a hot market like this."

I had an impulse to ask her if she would prefer to work in a slow market, but I did not want her to think I was making fun of her. Instead, I pointed out that, by giving so much mental attention to limitation and lack, she was attracting those qualities. Of course she was not drawing buyers to her. She broadcast inadequacy.

I told Deborah to make it a point to suggest constructive statements many times a day to her subconscious. I had my secretary print out a card for her with the following state-ments, which she was to meditate on every time she had an unoccupied moment:

> I have perfect faith in God's supply and in God's guidance. I know that all who buy a house through me are prospered and blessed. Infinite Intelligence attracts buyers to me who want the houses I sell, who can afford to buy them, and who will rejoice in their possession. I am blessed, and they are blessed. I am strong in the Lord and in the power of His might. Divine activity and immediate, perfect results now take place in my life, and I give thanks for the miracles in my life.

By carrying this card with her and repeating these truths frequently, Deborah restored her confidence in her sales abil-ity. She began to sell, prosper, and expand along all lines. She came up to me after another lecture, a few weeks later, and said, "Miracles are happening in my life. I sold two houses in the seven-figure range in just this last week, and I have firm offers on three others."

God's blessings never cease. Open your mind and heart and receive all the wealth you could want for yourself.

MEDITATION FOR THE RICHES OF FAITH

Jesus said, "Thy faith hath made thee whole."

I positively believe in the Healing Power of God within me. My conscious and subconscious mind are in perfect agreement. I accept the statement of truth, which I positively affirm. The words I speak are words of spirit and they are truth.

I now decree that the Healing Power of God is transform-ing my whole body, making me whole, pure, and perfect. I be-lieve with a deep, inner certitude that my prayer of faith is being manifested now. I am guided by the Wisdom of God in all matters. The Love of God flows in transcendent beauty and loveliness into my mind and body, transforming, restoring, and energizing every atom of my being. I sense the peace that passeth understanding. God's Glory surrounds me, and I rest forever in the Everlasting arms.

⌒ CHAPTER POINTS TO REMEMBER ⌒

1. Emerson says to trust yourself: "Every heart vibrates to that iron string." Join up with God within you, realizing that all things are possible to God. Place absolute trust in this Presence to respond to your call and aid you in the fulfillment of your dreams.

2. You are unique. There is no one in all the world like you. You are endowed with your own particular qualities, abilities, and capacities. As you claim, "God reveals my true expression," doors will open up and you will be Divinely expressed and in your true place in life, doing what you love to do, Divinely happy and Divinely prospered.

3. Teach children that they are children of God and that God loves them and cares for them. Have them affirm these truths frequently, knowing that there will be an immediate response from the God-Presence within them and that God will reveal His wonders in a different way through each child. As you do this, they will grow in self-confidence and self-reliance.

4. Confidence means "with faith." Have faith that when you call on Infinite Intelligence it responds to you. You build up your faith when you realize that thoughts are creative; what you feel you attract, and what you imagine you become. Any idea felt as true will be impressed on your subconscious mind and come to pass. This knowledge gives you faith in the laws of your mind. Its practice will work wonders in your life.

5. A magic formula for building self-confidence and success is to look in the mirror in the morning and affirm: "If God be for me, who can be against me? I can do all things through the God-Power that strengthens." Make a habit of this. You will become full of self-confidence and faith in all things good, and wonders will happen in your life.

6. Insist on the best in life and the best will come into your life. Realize you are one with the Infinite, and the Infinite cannot fail.

7. You must have a workable faith. You must demonstrate your faith in God and all things good. It must appear in your home, in your relationships with people, in your finances. Faith without demonstration and results is dead. Have faith in the creative laws of your mind, which never fail and never change.

8. Conceive of yourself now as successful and wealthy. Imagine the reality of the state, and irrespective of seeming obstacles and difficulties, you will experience the result of your mental image. Your mental image is absolute monarch and king. As you give it your attention, faith, and confidence, it must come to pass.

9. There is always an answer. There is Someone who cares—that One who created you and the universe. Trust it. It is the one, the beautiful, and the good.

10. If you are trying to sell something, whether it be a house or a new idea, realize what you are seeking is also seeking you. Claim boldly that Infinite Intelligence attracts to you buyers who want what you are selling and who will prosper with it and be happy. They are blessed, and you are blessed. Claim Divine activity and realize that since God's blessings and God's riches never cease flowing

into your experience, miracles will happen in your life. The day will break for you, and all the shadows will flee away.

11. Repeat the meditation at the end of the chapter for the never-failing riches of faith.

How to Use the Amazing Law That Reveals All Money Secrets

The most basic law of the universe is love. Love is always outgoing. It emanates from the person outward. Love must have an object. You can fall in love with music, art, a great project, an enterprise, a science, or any other field of human endeavor. You can fall deeply in love with the great principles and eternal verities that never change. Love is the emotional attachment you develop to your ideal, your cause, your plan, or your profession.

Because Einstein loved the principles of mathematics, they revealed their secrets to him. That is what loves does. You can fall in love with the science of mind and it will reveal to you its secrets. How much do you want what you want? Do you want to leave your old ideas, the traditional view of things, and get new ideas, new imagery, and new viewpoints? If so, you must work to become open and receptive. Do you want good digestion? If you do, you must give up resentment and say good-bye to your pet peeves and grudges. Do you want wealth and success? If so, you must be willing to accept the riches within and without. You must realize that you are born to succeed, for the Infinite within you cannot fail. You have to leave your jealousies, your envies, and all of the false concepts you may have of God and enter into the joy of abundant and richer living.

How an Actor Proved the Riches of Love

Some years ago I went to a stage performance of Shakespeare's *Henry IV*. I was particularly struck by the performance of the actor who played Falstaff. He seemed to capture the childlike wisdom that is such an amazing feature of the role. I checked my program; his name was Drew W.

After the performance, I went backstage to compliment him. He was clearly pleased, but also seemed troubled. When he found out my profession, he gave an ironic laugh and said, "I wish we had you on staff. I know I could use some help." "In what way?" I asked. "Not with your acting, certainly. Your performance tonight was brilliant."

"Thanks for that," he said. "Would you believe that I spent the half hour before the opening curtain drowning in worry?"

I said, "It's not the first time I've heard of such things. Tell me about it."

"Oh, it's all very dull and ordinary," Drew said, looking away. "I start thinking that I'll mess up. I'm sure I'll blow my lines. Not just dry up, you understand. No, I imagine myself saying something so utterly stupid that I ruin the entire performance. If that happens, who'll want me? Will I ever get another role? How will I live? The stage is my whole life!"

When he finished expounding his fears, I said, "Drew, you've spent many years training your body, your voice, your facial expressions, your gestures, isn't that right?"

He shrugged. "Well, of course. That's part of preparing to act."

"You should put the same intensity and effort into training your mind," I told him. "You can be in charge of your thoughts, ideas, imagery, and responses. When you issue orders, they will be automatically obeyed. You can tell your mind to dwell, not on failure and defeat, but on the power of God within you. It is that power that informs your acting, as it does every moment of your life."

He Practiced a Victory Formula

After Drew finished taking off his stage makeup and changing into street clothes, we went out for coffee and continued our conversation.

"What you have to do," I explained, "is give your personal transformation the same attention you would give to preparing a new role. Create and run through a scene, as vividly as your trained abilities can manage. Imagine that you are meeting and getting to know your inner self for the first time and that this new acquaintance is the most wonderful person you have ever met."

"It sounds as if I'm liable to find myself falling in love," he said with a smile.

"Exactly!" I replied. "And don't hide your love. Declare it openly!"

I wrote out a declaration and handed it to him. "Affirm this three or four times a day," I said. "Put into it every ounce of conviction you can muster. And please let me know how it works out."

This is the affirmation he began to make:

I give all my allegiance, devotion and loyalty to the God-Self within, which is none other than my Higher-Self. I know that love of my Higher-Self means to have a healthy, reverent, wholesome respect for the Divinity within me, which is all-powerful and all-wise. I know that love of God is to give my supreme allegiance to the One Presence and Power within me. I know I can do all things through the God-Power that strengthens me. As I perform on stage, just as in my life off-stage, the Presence within me speaks directly and clearly to the

Presence within those who watch. I live the role I play; I feel
entranced, fascinated, and absorbed in the drama; and I hear
those I love and respect congratulating me. It is wonderful.

As Drew continued to affirm these truths, his thoughts of
failure vanished. He went on to win several awards for his
work and today is sought after by theater directors in Europe
as well as in America.

There is no fear in love. *Perfect love casteth out fear*
(I John 4:18).

She Discovered the Riches
of the Law of Love

I have known Margaret R., a physician who specializes in
treating allergies, for years. Recently, she told me about a patient of hers, an old friend, who had avoided paying her bill
for months. It now amounted to several thousand dollars.

"If she were in difficulties, I might have decided to let it
go, just write it off," Margaret said. "But I know she is very
successful in her field. She also has very substantial family resources. She probably spends more on eating out every month
than what she owes me."

"Did you speak to her about the matter?" I asked.

"Oh, yes," Margaret said. "I even managed to be nice
about it. You know, 'I was wondering if you'd forgotten . . .' It
didn't work. She got very huffy with me, said my fees were
out of line, the treatment didn't work, and so on and so on. I
listened for a while, then thanked her for sharing her feelings
and hung up."

"That must have been upsetting," I remarked sympathetically.

"Not really," Margaret replied thoughtfully. "I realized
that whatever she was dealing with, it had little or nothing to
do with me. For a moment I thought about turning her account over to a collection agency and washing my hands of

it. But I knew that would mean losing a friend. So instead I turned it over to the law of love. During my morning and evening meditation sessions, I affirmed that Dorothy is honest, loving, kind, and at peace, and that God's love and harmony saturates her whole being. I visualized her standing in front of me, handing me a check, and thanking me for my help."

"And did you get the result you hoped for?" I asked.

Margaret smiled. "I certainly did! A few days after I started the process, Dorothy appeared in my office. She apologized for her bad temper, paid me in full, and told me she was making a very generous contribution to a foundation I'm associated with that does research into allergies. Not only that, she took me to lunch at a very fine restaurant and picked up the check! You have to know Dorothy to realize how amazing that is."

Margaret had just proven in her own experience the riches of the law of love. Notice that she did not retaliate or criticize her friend in any way. She simply surrounded her with God's love and peace, and Divine right action took place.

The Riches of Love Never Fail

Love is an outreaching of the heart. It is goodwill to all. If you are working in an office, factory, or store, it pays you fabulous dividends to wish for all those around you health, happiness, peace, promotion, wealth, and all the blessings of life. As you radiate love and goodwill to all, and as you wish riches and promotion for them, you will at the same time bless and prosper yourself. Remember, what you wish for another, you wish for yourself, and what you withhold from another, you withhold from yourself.

You are the only thinker in your universe, and your thoughts are creative; therefore, it is plain common sense to have goodwill for others and to radiate love and all the blessings of life to them.

The president of a nationwide chain of specialty stores told me recently that 90 percent of those who are dismissed by his company are fired not for absenteeism, incompetence, or dishonesty, but because they are unable to get along well with their customers and coworkers.

Love is the fulfilling of the law (Romans 13:10). The love spoken of in the Bible is not a sentiment or a Hollywood confection. Love is the cohesive force that unites families and nations. It keeps the whole world and the galaxies in space moving rhythmically, harmoniously, and peacefully through eons of time. Love is the law of health, happiness, peace, prosperity, and of joyous and successful living. The children of love are harmony, health, peace, kindness, joy, honesty, integrity, justice, and laughter.

Begin now to radiate the blessings of life to all those around you and to all people everywhere. Salute the Divinity in the other and silently realize for him or her: "The riches of God are flowing through you." You will be amazed at how you prosper. Showers of blessings will be yours.

The Infinite Riches of Love's Healing Balm

The late Dr. Harry Gaze, who was a famous international lecturer on mental and spiritual laws, told of a man in London who was wasting away due to tuberculosis. This man's spiritual adviser discovered that he hated bankers, brokers, and all wealthy people. This feeling stemmed from an early childhood experience, when he had witnessed his father being dispossessed of their home because he defaulted in payment to the local banker. In response, the child generalized from the particular and hated all bankers and rich people.

His spiritual adviser told him to go down to the London Stock Exchange and stand for one hour on the street near the building. For every single person, man or woman, who passed by, he was to affirm: "God's love fills your soul. The riches of God are yours now." The man did as he was told, albeit reluctantly at first. He kept his bargain. As he consciously and deliberately expressed love and riches to all, it came back to him multiplied a hundredfold. According to Dr. Gaze, this man experienced a remarkable healing. X-rays and other tests by Harley Street specialists showed he was completely healed. This man later got a job in a prominent banking firm and became very successful. Divine love became alive in his heart, in his body, and also in his pocketbook.

The Riches in Loving Your Wife, Husband, and Children in the Right Way

Claim that your loved ones are alive with the love of God and that His love saturates and permeates their whole being. Picture them in your mind's eye surrounded by the light of God's love. Realize that this healing light of God's love enfolds, enwraps, encompasses, and illumines their minds and bodies. Wonders happen as you pray this way.

She Found the Healing Power of Love

"My kid sister is really unhappy," a friend told me. "Her skin is a mess. She's tried all kinds of lotions and medications, but nothing seems to help. She's so miserable about it that she doesn't even want to leave the house. Can you help?"

"I think so," I said. I found my mind turning to the words from the Bible: *His flesh shall be fresher than a child's: he shall return to the days of his youth* (Job 33:25).

We made a few appropriate changes in the verse. Beginning the next day, my friend's sister looked at herself in the mirror each morning while affirming,

> My skin is an envelope of God's love. It is without spot and blemish. It is fresher than a child's, and the radiance of youth and beauty saturate my whole being.

Her face cleared up in a few weeks. It is now as soft and beautiful as she desired, as it radiates the sunshine of God's love.

The Riches of Love Bring Justice in a Lawsuit

Vincent G. came to me full of frustration. He was the defendant in a civil suit that had dragged on for years, tying up his resources and attention. He could talk of nothing except the unfair judges, the unscrupulous attorneys, and the witnesses whose depositions were full of deliberate lies.

"I can't afford to settle this thing," he concluded. "But I can't afford to go on like this, either. It's taken over my whole life. I don't know what to do."

"The approach you've been following obviously hasn't worked for you," I observed. "Why don't you try something very different?"

At my suggestion, Vincent began to pray night and morning as follows:

> All those involved in this suit are surrounded by the sacred circle of God's love. God's love, truth, and harmony reign supreme in the minds and hearts of all involved. They are all known in Divine mind, and the law of love prevails.

This prayer dissolved all bitterness, resentment, and hostility lodged in his subconscious mind, which then manifested a solution in Divine order.

A few weeks later, the plaintiff in the suit was arrested on an unrelated charge. In interrogation, he admitted having fabricated the documents that supported the suit against Vincent. Shortly afterward, the man's attorneys abandoned the suit.

The Riches of the Protecting Power of Love

Howard R. is a psychiatrist whose office is in the same building as mine. Recently, I ran into him in the corridor and noticed his ashen face.

"What a day!" he exclaimed. "This morning one of my patients pulled out a pistol, pointed it at my head, and told me that he had orders from God to kill me."

I stared at him in horror. "What on earth did you do?" I asked.

"I managed to stay calm," he said. "I told him, 'God must have changed his mind, because He told me this morning what to do to heal you.' When I saw him waver, I added, 'God indwells you and God indwells me. God can't contradict Himself. God is love, and He wants you whole and perfect now.' At that point, he handed me the gun and burst into tears. He's now on his way to a mental hospital, where I'll be able to give him more intensive treatment. My hope is that this crisis will be a turning point in a good direction."

As a spiritual-minded person, Dr. R. knew that his contemplation of God's Presence in the patient would be felt by him. *Perfect love casteth out fear* (I John 4:18).

Love Unites and Love Heals

The members of your family and others close to you have a deep need to feel loved, wanted, appreciated, and important in the scheme of things. I was recently consulted by an attorney, Mark L., who confessed, "I've been having an affair for the last year with someone in my firm. It's crazy. I love my wife and kids, and here I am, halfway down the road to losing them."

"Why?" I asked. "What is the attraction of this affair?"

"Caitlin makes me feel important," he replied. "She's a top-notch lawyer herself, but she always praises my accomplishments and tells me how wonderful I am, how brilliant I am, what a marvelous conversationalist I am, and how clever and brilliant I am in my field. I know it's flattery, but it works. She makes me feel like a king."

I asked him, "What about your wife?"

"She's wonderful," he said. "She's loyal, devoted, sincere, and a marvelous mother. But . . . well, I'm nobody when I go home. I get no recognition. She nags me."

I explained to him that many people nag because they get no appreciation, attention, and praise. Moreover, your wife or husband subconsciously detects your infidelity. When we feel something valued slipping away, we are tempted to grab at it.

Mark was clear that he did not want a divorce. I brought him and his wife together. After a long and heartfelt discussion, they realized that the love they felt for each other was still there but dormant and never openly expressed. For years neither of them had clearly manifested his or her love for the other. They took each other for granted.

To preserve the marriage, both began a prayer process, he with the 91st Psalm every night and she with the 27th Psalm every morning. Both made a commitment to radiate love, peace, and harmony to each other regularly and systematically. Each agreed to affirm for the other five minutes every day: "God's love fills your soul. I love you."

Love united them again in a Divine embrace, for love is the universal solvent. Only God and His love can and do heal the wounds of mankind.

MEDITATION: LOVE AND GOODWILL PROSPER ME

All ye are brethren, for one is your father. (Matthew 23:8–9) I bring harmony, peace, and joy into every situation and into all of my personal relationships. I know, believe, and claim that the peace of God reigns supreme in the mind and heart of everyone in my home and business. No matter what the problem is, I always maintain peace, poise, patience, and wisdom. I fully and freely forgive everyone, regardless of what they may have said or done. I cast all my burdens on the God-self within. I go free. This is a marvelous feeling. I know that blessings come to me as I forgive.

I see the angel of God's Presence behind every problem or difficult situation. I know the solution is there and that everything is working out in Divine order. I trust the God Presence implicitly. It knows how to accomplish what must be done. The Absolute Order of Heaven and His Absolute Wisdom are acting through me now and at all times. I know that order is Heaven's first law.

My mind is now fixed joyously and expectantly on this perfect harmony. I know the result is the inevitable, perfect solution; my answer is God's answer; for it is Divine.

➢ CHAPTER POINTS TO REMEMBER ➢

1. Love is always outgoing. Love frees; it gives; it is the spirit of God in action. Love must have an object. You can fall in love with music, art, science, mathematics, or the truths of God. You can also fall in love with your Higher-Self by recognizing it as the source of all blessings. It is God in you.

2. You are the king and absolute monarch over your thoughts, images, ideas, and responses. You can order your thoughts around like an employer instructing employees what to do. You can steer your thoughts correctly in the same way you steer your car.

3. Love of your Higher-Self, or God, means you have a healthy, reverent, wholesome respect for the Divinity within you, which is all-powerful, all-wise, knows all and sees all. You give supreme allegiance to the Spirit within you, which is God, and you absolutely refuse to give power to any created thing.

4. You can fall in love with a grander, greater, nobler concept of yourself by imagining you are doing what you love to do. Become absorbed and engrossed in the mental movie and you will achieve your goal. Love of your ideal casts out all fear.

5. In the midst of an emergency, affirm: "The Lord is my light and my salvation; whom shall I fear? The Lord is the strength of my life; of whom shall I be afraid?" There will be a response and security will be yours.

6. When a person is abusive and refuses to pay a just debt, surround that person with light and love; feel and know that the love of God flows through the person and that the law of harmony prevails. A harmonious solution follows.

7. Radiate love, peace, and goodwill to all people around you and to all people everywhere. Wish for them health, happiness, peace, abundance and all the blessings of life. As you make a habit of this, countless blessings will be yours. Ninety percent of people who are failures in life don't get ahead because they rub others the wrong way. Love and goodwill is the answer.

8. Love is the fulfilling of the law of health, happiness, wealth, and success. Love is goodwill to all, and what you wish for another you wish for yourself.

9. If resentful of others' wealth and success, affirm for everyone you see and meet: "God's love fills your soul and the riches of God are yours now." Wonders will happen in

your life. You will be healed of jealousy and ill will, and you will prosper.

10. If married, tell your wife or husband, "I love you. God loves you." Feel it; believe it; proclaim it. Love unites and preserves the marriage.

11. If you have skin trouble, affirm: "My skin is an envelope of God's love and is without spot and blemish." Realize that Divine love dissolves everything unlike itself, and your skin will become whole, radiant and perfect.

12. If involved in a protracted and complicated lawsuit of any kind, realize that God's love flows through the minds and hearts of all involved and that there is a Divine solution through the harmony and love of God. See the happy ending and contemplate the Divine solution through the action of God's love, and victory and right action will be yours.

13. You can protect yourself by realizing God's love in the other and God's love saturating and surrounding you. Realize it is God talking to God, and you will be protected and set free.

14. To preserve a marriage, see God in each other and exalt God in one another, and the marriage will grow more blessed through the years. Love unites. Love heals. Love restores the soul. God is love.

15. Use the meditation at the end of the chapter to manifest all kinds of riches in daily living.

How to Charge Yourself with Money-Magnetism

Ralph Waldo Emerson said, "Nothing can bring you peace but the triumph of principles." When you learn the way your mind works and direct it wisely, you will add to your peace, prosperity, poise, balance, and security.

The engineer who is building a bridge follows the principles of mathematics in his work. He draws on the knowledge he has gained of stresses, strains, and the characteristics of materials. These are based on immutable laws that are the same yesterday, today, and forever.

In a similar way, the laws of mind are immutable. You can gain a working knowledge of them from the Bible, which says: *As thou hast believed, so be it done unto thee* (Matthew 8:13).

Excess tension interferes with the productive lives of thousands of people, bringing about frustration and many nervous disorders in its train. A certain amount of anxiety is normal and necessary. For example, the singer about to go on the stage is somewhat tense. This is properly understood as an accumulation of energy and power that charges her mental and spiritual batteries, enabling her to overcome any sense of anticipated failure. What is dangerous is excessive and prolonged tension. When the singer begins to sing, she ticks off that surplus energy in the same manner as a clock that is wound up ticks off the time. If you wind the clock too tightly, you break the spring, and then we have no song or time, either.

When you charge yourself with the feeling that you can do all things through the God-Power that strengthens you, you will give a wonderful performance.

How an Entrepreneur Overcame Tension and Anxiety over Her Debts

On the plane to Las Vegas recently, I got into a conversation with Maria S., the founder and CEO of a Net-based electronics mall. She told me that not long after starting her company, she ran into a very severe cash flow problem. Her suppliers started pressing her for payment and cut off shipments to her. It looked as if her whole operation was about to go down the tubes.

"One night when things looked darkest," she said, "I picked up my Bible. It fell open to the 23rd Psalm. An idea welled up inside me. I sat down and made a list of all those to whom I owed money. I put down each name, along with the exact amount I owed them. Then in my imagination I visited each one and handed him or her a check for the full amount I owed. In my mind's eye, I saw each one smile and thank me for being so responsible. I felt the handshake of each one, saw the happy look on each face, and heard each one say that my credit is good any time."

She added that she followed this procedure every night, with as much vividness as possible, feeling the naturalness and joy of it all. Each time, when she finished her prayer process, she felt a great sense of peace and tranquility. At the end of about two weeks, she had a very vivid dream, in which a disembodied hand led her into a particular casino and to one of the roulette tables, then indicated a certain series of numbers on the wheel. When she awakened, she wrote down the numbers. That same evening, she did exactly as she recalled from the dream. In less than half an hour, she won more than enough to pay off all her debts. She has not gambled since and says she never will. The wisdom of her subconscious had responded in its own unique way to her request.

How to Banish Anxiety over Debts

Over the years, I have given the following prayer to many people who are burdened with debts and have unpaid bills piling up on them:

> God is the Source of my supply. I know when I am anxious, it means I do not trust God. The money I now possess is magnified and multiplied a thousandfold. I realize all the money I have is a symbol of the infinite riches of God. I turn to the Infinite Presence within, knowing in my heart and soul it opens the way for me to pay all my debts, leaving me a vast surplus. I surrender a list of all these debts in the hands of my Heavenly Father, and I give thanks they are all paid in Divine order. God's riches are circulating in my life, and I rejoice and am exceedingly glad that every creditor is paid now, and God prospers me beyond my fondest dreams. I believe that I have received now, and I know that according to my faith is it done unto me. I know God will rain blessings from Heaven for me now.

I tell those in debt to claim these truths joyously, lovingly, and with the understanding that there is always a response in accordance with their request. When anxious thoughts come to mind, they are never to think of bills or lack or debts, but smilingly to give thanks for God's abundance and riches and rejoice that the obligation is paid now. When this technique is followed faithfully, there is a reconditioning of the mind to wealth, and I have seen marvelous results follow. You can apply this prayer process and let wonders happen in your life.

Learn to Relax and Let Go and Experience Riches All Around You

It is not hard to believe in the Invisible Source of supply. Your five senses reveal to you the world around you on this three-dimensional plane. Your ears are attuned to hear only a few octaves of sound, yet your radio and television reveal to you that all about you, unhearable with your naked senses, are symphonies, music, laughter, songs, drama, speeches, and voices from thousands of miles away.

Your eyes are geared to see the physical objects around you, but the atmosphere is also full of images, invisible to the eye, of movie stars, historical events, comedies, tragedies, and, of course, endless commercials. You do not see gamma rays, beta rays, alpha waves, radio waves, and cosmic rays, yet the atmosphere is nevertheless teeming with these vibrations.

Your thought-image of wealth, money, and property, which you don't see, is prior to that idea and causes it. By accepting this truth and feeling the reality of it, your invisible thought-image will become money, riches, or whatever you need. Thoughts are things.

How a Secretary Overcame Anxiety and Tension in the Office

"I've come to dread going to work every morning," Lisa A. told me during a consultation. She had already told me that she was an executive secretary with a major law firm. "There is so much strife and contention and backbiting among the staff. I try not to pay attention, but all the intrigue really undermines me. Well, not just me, everybody. It's terrible!"

"It's very hard to work in that kind of atmosphere," I agreed. "But what you should understand is that no one can really disturb you but yourself. It is your reaction to what is going on, the movement of your own thoughts, that bothers you. And *you* command your thoughts, no one else does.

Your serenity and inner peace can be an umbrella that sheds all the negative energy others try to pour over you."

I went on to explain that the suggestions, statements, and actions of others have no power to disturb or annoy you unless you transfer the power in yourself to them and tell yourself, "He or she has power to irritate me." If you do that, you are enthroning false gods in your mind. Your harmony, peace, health, or wealth is not dependent on others. Enthrone God in your mind. Let God be your employer, boss, paymaster, adjuster, and troubleshooter.

I suggested to Lisa that she use the following spiritual formula regularly:

> God's love governs me at work. I have no opinion about others. I judge not; therefore, I cannot suffer or be disturbed. The peace and harmony of God govern me and all that I do. Every anxious thought is completely stilled, for I am working for God, and His peace fills my soul. The confidence and joy of God enfold me at all times. All who work in the office are God's sons and daughters, and each one contributes to the peace, harmony, prosperity, and success of this office. Divine love comes in the door of our office; and Divine love governs the minds and hearts of all in the office; and Divine love goes out the door. God is my boss, my paymaster, my guide, and my counselor, and I recognize no other. I give all power and recognition to God and I walk serenely and peacefully in His light. I laugh, I sing, and I rejoice. God works wonders in my life.

Lisa repeated this prayer every morning before going to work and every night before going to sleep. She quickly built up an immunity to all negative suggestions and thoughts from those around her. When someone was obnoxious, surly, or sarcastic, she would silently say to herself, "I salute the Divinity in you. God thinks, speaks, and acts through you." Nothing bothered her, nothing moved her, nothing disturbed her, and nothing frightened her. She had found God within herself, and that was sufficient. Knowing how to pray paid her fabulous dividends. It will do the same for you.

How a Student Overcame His Anxiety That He Would Fail His Examinations

Jack R., a college senior, sat in my office with his hands clasped tightly in his lap. "I just know I'm going to flunk out," he told me. "I hit the books every night, but by the next day, I don't remember a thing. Every time I take an exam, I clutch up like you wouldn't believe. I've tried studying my Bible regularly, but it doesn't seem to help. What can I do? If I bomb college, it'll kill my parents."

I told Jack that the root of his trouble was that ongoing feeling of anxiety and tension. He goes to class afraid he can't remember and to exams afraid he will fail. In that state of stress, the mind establishes a block. The information he needs is stored in his subconscious mind, but the stress keeps it from being accessed by the surface mind.

I gave a spiritual formula, suggesting that every night, before beginning to study, he pray and affirm the following:

> *Acquaint now thyself with him, and be at peace: thereby good shall come unto thee* (Job 22:21). *When he giveth quietness, who then can make trouble?* (Job 34:29). *For thus saith the Lord God, the Holy One of Israel; In returning and rest shall ye be saved; in quietness and in confidence shall be your strength* (Isaiah 30:15). *For God is not the author of confusion, but of peace* (I Corinthians 14:33). *Great peace have they which love thy law; and nothing shall offend them* (Psalm 119:165).

He saturated his mind every night with these great truths, absorbing and mentally digesting them. He imagined these truths sinking into his subconscious mind like seeds deposited in the soil and becoming a part of him. He made a mental adjustment and focused his attention on God's river of peace and power and no longer fixed his attention on his problems.

His mind now stayed on God. Just before going to sleep every night, he affirmed, "I have a perfect memory for everything I need to know. I pass all examinations in Divine order, and I give thanks." He is now on top of his problem and is relaxed mentally, spiritually, and physically. His anxieties have been lifted, and his talent and memory are set free. As he saturated his mind with these age-old biblical truths, he neutralized all the negative patterns in his subconscious mind and became transformed by the renewal of his mind.

How an Executive Overcame Anxiety over His Business Situation

I recently spoke with Ron W., an executive in the entertainment industry, who told me his doctor had diagnosed him as suffering from "anxiety neurosis." He added that he was terribly tense, suffered from insomnia, and was constantly worried about money and the future.

I explained to him that a certain amount of tension is good. For example, steel without tension would not be considered good steel. I added that what his doctor meant is undoubtedly abnormally misdirected tension or energy. I suggested that he cooperate with his doctor, but I also urged him to practice the great therapy of words.

The way Ron overcame his anxiety neurosis was as follows. He began to have meditation sessions with himself three or four times a day, at which times he affirmed quietly and lovingly:

> My feet are relaxed, my ankles are relaxed, the calves of my legs are relaxed, my abdominal muscles are relaxed, my heart and lungs are relaxed, my spine is relaxed, my neck and shoulders are relaxed, my brain is relaxed, my eyes are relaxed, my hands and arms are relaxed. My whole being is relaxed. I feel God's river of peace flowing through me like a golden river of life, love, truth, and beauty. The spirit and inspiration of the Almighty flow through me, vitalizing, healing, and restoring my entire being. The wisdom and power of the Almighty enable me to fulfill all my goals in Divine order through Divine love. I am always relaxed, serene, poised, and balanced, and my

faith and confidence is in God and all things good. I can do all things through the God-Power that strengthens me. I dwell in the secret place of the Most High, and all the thoughts entertained by me conform to harmony, peace, and goodwill to all. *For God hath not given us the spirit of fear; but of power, and of love, and of a sound mind* (II Timothy 1:7). I sleep in peace, and I wake in joy. God supplies all my needs, and His riches flow freely into my experience. My security is in God and His love.

Ron reiterated these truths frequently during the day, and these wonderful spiritual vibrations neutralized and obliterated the disease-soaked anxiety center in his subconscious mind. His two favorite words became "serenity and tranquility." He discovered there were spiritual reserves on which he could call to annihilate all the anxious and worried thoughts. He now has a deep faith in all things good. He has discovered that peace is the power at the heart of God. *And let the peace of God rule in your hearts* (Colossians 3:15).

MEDITATION FOR BEING IN THE PRESENCE OF INFINITE RICHES

The following meditation has performed wonders for people for richer living and continuing prosperity:

Today I am reborn spiritually! I completely detach myself from the old way of thinking, and I bring Divine love, light, and truth definitely into my experience. I consciously feel love for everyone I meet. Mentally I say to everyone I contact, "I see the God in you and I know you see the God in me." I recognize the qualities of God in everyone. I practice this morning, noon, and night; it is a living part of me.

I am reborn spiritually now, because all day long I practice the Presence of God. No matter what I am doing—whether I am walking the street, shopping, or going about my daily business—whenever my thought wanders away from God or the good, I bring it back to the contemplation of His Holy Presence: I feel noble, dignified, and God-like. I walk in a high mood sensing my oneness with God. His peace fills my soul.

☞ CHAPTER POINTS TO REMEMBER ☜

1. Nothing can bring you peace but the triumph of principles. Use your mind the right way by feeding it with God-like ideas, and you will experience serenity and tranquility. Think right, feel right, act right, do right, and pray right.

2. A certain amount of tension is good. Excess tension is destructive. If you wind your clock too tightly, you break the spring. For any important assignment or performance, you accumulate a certain amount of energy, which is the power of God in you. It enables you to give a marvelous performance; and like a well-oiled clock, you tick the energy off rhythmically, harmoniously, and joyously. Excess tension is fear and anxiety. Contemplate the peace of God flowing through you and the power of the Almighty strengthening you, and the anxiety and fear will be rendered null and void.

3. When you have a lot of unpaid bills, do not dwell on what you owe. Claim God is your instant supply, meeting all your financial needs now. Write down the names of all the creditors and the amounts you owe each one, and give thanks that they are paid in full now. Imagine you are giving each one a check and that they are smiling and congratulating you. Do it over and over again until you feel the tones of reality.

4. Rejoice and be exceedingly glad in your mind that every creditor is paid now and that God's wealth is circulating in your life, that you are prospered beyond your fondest dreams. Believe; rejoice; give thanks, for He never faileth.

5. Realize that everything you look at in this universe came out of the invisible mind of God or man. Your thought-image of wealth causes wealth, in the same way that your computer, car, or home began as thought-images in the mind of the engineer or builder.

6. No one can disturb you but yourself. It is not what people say or do that annoys you; it is your own reaction or your thought about it. Where there is no opinion, there is no suffering. Keep your eyes on the God-Presence within you and give your allegiance, loyalty, and confidence to the Supreme Cause within you. Stop worshipping false gods. With your eyes stayed on God, there is no evil on your pathway. God is your boss, your paymaster, your guide, and your counselor, and you give all honor and glory to Him.

7. Excess tension and anxiety interfere with your memory and efficiency along all lines. The ideal way to get a quiet mind is to identify with the great eternal truths of the Bible and reiterate these spiritual gems of wisdom. By osmosis, they will penetrate the subconscious mind, and you will find yourself relaxed and at peace. One of these spiritual pearls is *Thou wilt keep him in perfect peace, whose mind is stayed on thee, because he trusteth in thee* (Isaiah 26:3).

8. When you are tense, anxious, jittery, and worried, dwell on this great truth: *For God hath not given us the spirit of fear; but of power, and of love, and of a sound mind* (II Timothy 1:7). If you are an insomniac, affirm prior to sleep: "I sleep in peace, I wake in joy, and I live in God." *When thou liest down, thou shalt not be afraid; yea, thou shalt lie down, and thy sleep shall be sweet.* (Proverbs 3:24).

9. Use the meditation at the end of the chapter to ease tension and anxiety and to realize the God in everyone.

How to Automatically Reap an Abundant Harvest of Golden Blessings

As I have already pointed out, the key to self-confidence is given by Emerson in his work on self-reliance: "Trust thyself: every heart vibrates to that iron string . . . Great men have always done so . . . betraying their perception that the absolute trustworthy was seated at their heart, working through their hands, predominating in all thinking."

Great numbers of men and women do not trust themselves; they demean and lower themselves. The real Self of everyone is God, which Emerson refers to as the absolute trustworthy seated in your heart. The Divine presence is lodged in your own subjective depths, governing your entire body, watching over you even when you are sound asleep. It is the unseen power that moves your hands and that enables you to walk and talk, revealing to you everything you need to know. All that is required of you is that you trust this Presence and Power, and the answer will be yours. The place of contact and acquaintance is within yourself.

How to Build Self-Confidence

Self-confidence comes when you realize God, which Emerson calls the absolute trustworthy, is in your own subjective depths. Affirm frequently:

> God indwells me, walks and talks with me. God is guiding me now. I can do all things through the God-Power that strengthens me. If God be for me, who can be against me? There is no power to challenge God, and God watches over me in all my ways. I realize every problem is Divinely out-matched and I grapple courageously with every assignment, knowing that God reveals the answer. God loves me and cares for me.

Every morning and every evening, become mentally absorbed with the beauty and wisdom of these truths, and gradually they will take possession of you, penetrating your subconscious mind, and you will move through the vicissitudes of life with an abiding faith and confidence, plus a feeling of victory over all problems.

How Self-Confidence Brought a Young Man Riches

While filling a prescription recently, I got into a conversation with the young pharmacist. I noticed that the last name on his license was the same as the name of the drugstore. "Is this a family business?" I asked.

"Not exactly," he replied. "Until two years ago, I was working on salary for one of the big drugstore chains. But the manager and I didn't get along. Frankly, he wanted me to cut a few corners that I didn't think were ethical. He finally fired me on grounds of incompetence."

"How awful," I remarked.

He smiled. "Not at all! It turned out to be the luckiest day of my life. I told myself when it happened that only good could come of it, because I know that Infinite Intelligence guides, directs, and reveals the next step to me. I felt a deep, intuitive urge to talk over what had happened with my father-in-law. He was outraged and said that he was so confident in my abilities that he would lend me the money to buy my own pharmacy."

"And here you are," I said, looking around the bright, up-to-date facility.

"Not exactly," he said again. "My pharmacy did such a volume of business that I was able to pay back my father-in-law and make a down payment on a second store. This is it."

This young pharmacist believes in the Self within him and in his ability to succeed. His self-confidence has paid him great dividends, not only in money, but in poise, assurance, and a rare sense of humor. Remember, self-confidence is contagious; it is communicated subjectively to others who aid you in the realization of your heart's desire.

His Self-Confidence Dissolved His Lack of Funds

The late Dr. Olive Gaze, an associate of mine, told me about a man who came to her very bitter and hostile to his two brothers, who had cheated him out of a large sum of money. He was in financial straits and panicky as a result.

She instructed him to place his confidence in the Source and to release his brothers from his hatred as follows:

> I surrender my brothers to God completely. I have confidence that God is the eternal Source of my supply. God's love fills my soul. God's peace saturates my mind and heart. I have supreme confidence in God's guidance and directions. I am strong in the Lord and in the power of His might. God's wealth flows to me freely, joyously and endlessly. I give thanks for God's riches now.

As he planted these seeds of love and confidence, all bitterness within him was dissolved. He had been taking care of his grandmother, who was very old and feeble and did not want to go to a retirement home. He visited her twice a day and saw to it that she was provided for. He got her groceries, paid her bills, and drove her to church on Sundays, all the time thinking that she was living on a meager pension plus Social Security. He was motivated entirely by kindness and love. He did not expect or look for any reward.

His grandmother passed on suddenly one evening. To his great surprise, an attorney called to tell him that her entire estate had been left to him. The value of the estate was several hundred thousand dollars, much more than the amount he had been cheated out of by his brothers. His confidence in the Source of all blessings, plus his giving of love, forgiveness, and goodwill, brought him an abundant harvest.

Building Self-Confidence Prior to Going to Sleep

One of the best times to develop self-confidence is at bedtime, when you are in a sleepy, drowsy, relaxed state. In such a state, the boundary of your subconscious mind is more easily crossed, which makes it one of the best times to instill new ideas that impregnate your deeper mind. During the sleep period, these ideas gestate in the darkness of your mind, and your deeper mind determines the best way to bring riches, prosperity, and success to you.

A business executive named Roger P. confessed to me that he was plagued with the fear of failure and bankruptcy. He was putting off his creditors as best he could, but he did not think he could keep it up much longer. I gave him the following thoughts of confidence, wealth, and success to be affirmed slowly, quietly, and feelingly every night prior to sleep:

I sleep in peace every night, and I wake in joy and confidence, knowing that God is guiding me and reveals the perfect plan for the fulfillment of my desires. My business is God's business, and God's business always prospers. God's wealth circulates in my life and there is always a surplus. I am consistently attracting to me more and more customers, and every day of my life I am giving greater service. All my employees are blessed and have prospered, and happiness, prosperity, and the riches of God reign supreme in the minds and hearts of all. I am full of confidence and absolute trust in my senior partner, which is God.

Roger practiced this prayer-therapy technique every night. As he charged his subconscious with these life-giving patterns, he found his whole life and business patterns changing. A multinational corporation that was expanding into his line of business offered an advantageous buy-out for cash and stock. He was delighted to sell and cleared far more than he would have expected. He was able to pay off all his debts and retire to Hawaii.

The ways of your Divine inner mind are past finding out. Like Roger, you can prove to yourself that your subconscious magnifies exceedingly that which you deposit in it.

The Riches of a New Estimate of Yourself

Approve of yourself. Accept yourself. Realize that you are a unique, individualized expression of God. You are a son or daughter of the Living God. The basis of your new understanding of yourself is a deep conviction in the Supreme Intelligence within you, which always responds to your thought. Place your faith in that which never changes but which is the same yesterday, today, and forever. Theologies, governments, philosophies, and political systems wax and wane; floods come and go; everything changes and passes away in this universe. But when you place your confidence in the Life-Principle within you, you will never want for any good thing. Whatever means of exchange may come into use, you will always have all you need as well as a Divine surplus.

Remember these great truths: *I will fear no evil: for thou art with me* (Psalm 23:4) and *For he shall give his angels charge over thee, to keep thee in all thy ways* (Psalm 91:11).

She Found That the Riches of Self-Confidence Dissolved Her Inferiority Complex

As I was buying a new shirt in a department store, I asked the young woman who was helping me if she thought the color and pattern would look good on me.

A look of alarm crossed her face. "Oh, please, don't ask me," she said hastily. "I don't know anything about that. I'd better get my supervisor."

Surprised, I glanced at her name badge, then said, "Well, Sally, I don't think that's necessary. I just wanted your opinion. You don't have to be an expert to have an opinion."

"I'm sorry," she said. "I'm just so ignorant. I didn't have the advantage of a college education. Let me go find somebody who'll be more help to you."

"You don't have to feel so bad just because you didn't go to college," I said. "We all have strengths we don't use because we don't acknowledge them. The things that have happened to you, including your education, are the results of your ideas about yourself. If you change your ideas, you will change what happens to you as well."

"I'd love to believe that," Sally sighed. "But I don't even know where to start."

We arranged for her to come to my office after work, and I finished buying my shirt. During our consultation later that day, I suggested to Sally that she begin by frequently declaring the following truths:

> I am a daughter of God. I am unique; there is no one in all the world like me, because God never repeats Himself. God is my Father and I am His child. God loves me and cares for me. Any time I am prone to criticize or find fault with myself, I will immediately affirm: "I exalt God in the midst of me." God is now expressing Himself in a wonderful way through me. I radiate love, peace, and goodwill to all. I am one with my Father, and my Father is God. I know the real Self of me is God, and from this moment forward, I have a healthy, reverent respect for the Divinity within me, which created me and gave me life, breath, and all things.

As she meditated on these truths, she found all sense of insecurity and inferiority vanish. She began to think quietly of the kind of career she would like to have. She began to take evening courses in information management and soon found herself promoted to a managerial position in the store. She became acquainted shortly thereafter with one of her coworkers who also suffered from a lack of self-confidence. In the course of helping him to recognize his own relationship to Divinity, she fell in love. Today they enjoy all the riches of a harmonious, spiritual, and prosperous marriage. Because she got in touch with the riches within her, she found the riches of life manifested on the screen of space.

Benefits of Practicing the Riches of Praise

Robbie M. is the son of an old friend. He came to me one day and confided that his professor had suggested he join a class in calculus, but he was afraid to do it.

"I'm sure I'll be totally lost," he added. "I just don't have the background."

"Robbie, I don't buy that," I replied. "I can't imagine your professor would be urging this if he didn't have confidence and trust in your ability. What's much more important, Infinite Intelligence is within you. You are wise enough to know that it always responds to you. You have what it takes, if you only trust in it. . . . With your faith in God and His laws of mind, I have perfect confidence that you can do it, and I want you to accept the offer at once. God will guide you in your studies and reveal to you everything you need to know."

Robbie beamed with delight at my confidence and praise. Today, he is the top student in his calculus class, and he is beginning to consider doing graduate work in the field.

What Robbie needed was someone to stir up his confidence and appreciation of his Higher Self. Remember, whole-souled confidence in the Self of you and of others will bring about miracles in your life and in theirs.

A Husband Discovers the Riches of Calling Forth Confidence in His Wife

"My wife is brilliant, but her academic career is going nowhere," Adam W. told me. I already knew that he was a rising attorney and that his wife, Anne, taught art history at a prestigious college.

"Why do you think that is?" I asked.

"Pure lack of ambition," he replied. "It drives me wild to see people who don't have half her qualifications being promoted and honored while she gets ignored. If only she didn't feel so inadequate. I've talked to her until I'm blue in the face, but I can't see that it's done a bit of good."

"Maybe it's time for a new approach," I said. I suggested that instead of talking to her, he try the silent method. I explained. Three or four times a day, for about five minutes each time, he was to make a confident and sincere declaration of his wife's untapped abilities. "When you do," I concluded, "your wife will receive your affirmations subjectively. Her subconscious mind will compel her to express her latent powers."

Adam agreed. He began that same afternoon to make the following affirmation:

> My wife is a tremendous success. She is absolutely outstanding. The Infinite within her is all-wise and all-powerful. My wife is going from glory to glory; she is going up the ladder of success and promotion. Her real talents are revealed and appreciated. She is Divinely guided and her success comes to pass now. I give thanks, for I know what I decree stirs up the gift of God within her.

Within three months' time, Anne had a major paper accepted for publication and was promoted to a tenure-bearing position. She also received a prestigious grant to spend a summer in Italy pursuing her research on a long-neglected Renaissance painter. She is manifesting in outer reality her husband's inner conviction of her abilities.

MEDITATION FOR BUILDING SELF-CONFIDENCE

> I know that the answer to my problem lies in the God-Self within me. I now become quiet, still, and relaxed. I am at peace. I know God speaks in peace and not in confusion. I am now in tune with the Infinite; I know and believe implicitly that Infinite Intelligence is revealing to me the perfect answer. I think about the solution to my problems. I now live in the mood I would have were my problem solved. I truly live in this abiding faith and trust that is the mood of the solution; this is the spirit of God moving within me. This Spirit is omnipotent; it is manifesting itself; my whole being rejoices in the solution; I am glad. I live in this feeling and give thanks.

I know that God has the answer. With God all things are possible. God is the Living Spirit Almighty within me; He is the source of all wisdom and illumination.

The indicator of the Presence of God within me is a sense of peace and poise. I now cease all sense of strain and struggle; I trust the God-Power implicitly. I know that all the wisdom and power I need to live a glorious and successful life are within me. I relax my entire body; my faith is in His wisdom; I go free. I claim and feel the peace of God flooding my mind, heart, and whole being. I know the quiet mind gets its problems solved. I now turn the request over to the God-Presence knowing it has an answer. I am at peace.

☙ CHAPTER POINTS TO REMEMBER ☙

1. Emerson said, "Trust thyself; every heart vibrates to that iron string. The absolutely trustworthy is seated in your own heart." To know that God indwells you, walks and talks in you, and responds to your thoughts gives you confidence and faith in that which never fails.

2. You build self-confidence by knowing that the God-Power in you is almighty. There is nothing to oppose omnipotence, nothing to challenge it, and when your thoughts are God's thoughts, God's power is with your thoughts of good. Realize that God loves you and cares for you, and then all sense of insecurity and fear goes away.

3. If you are fired from a position, don't get depressed or angry, but realize the God-Presence within you will open up a new door of expression for you in Divine order, and you will experience the joy of the answered prayer.

4. Place your confidence in God, the source of all blessings. As you call upon it, the answer comes. Claim, "God's wealth is circulating in my life and God is guiding me." If resentment is present toward any person, release that

person, wishing for him or her all the blessings of life. As you fill your mind and heart with Divine love, all bitterness and resentment is dissolved and your good will flow to you.

5. Practice conveying ideas of prosperity, success, and wealth to your subconscious prior to sleep. As you make a habit of this, you will establish patterns of wealth and success in your life, and the powers of your subconscious being compulsive, you will find yourself compelled to express the riches of God in all areas. You will find that unseen forces hasten to minister to your eternal good.

6. Approve of yourself. You are a child of the Infinite and heir to all the riches of life. The Self of you is God. Honor and exalt the God-Presence within you. Know, believe, and practice aligning yourself mentally with the God-Presence within you, knowing that it will respond to you and take care of you all the days of your life. You will experience riches and peace in this changing world.

7. All inferiority disappears as you contemplate that God is your Father and that He loves you and cares for you. Whenever you are prone to denigrate or demean yourself, affirm: "I exalt God in the midst of me." As you make a habit of this, all sense of self-rejection and inferiority disappears. As you practice this technique, God will flow through you, filling up all the empty vessels in your life.

8. As you praise the qualities, powers, talents, and abilities in others, they will rise to the occasion and you will find that they really stir up the gifts of God within them. Praise is a miracle-working power. Practice it.

9. You can convey the riches of silent praise to your husband, wife, or others close to you. There is no time or space in mind, and as you affirm with feeling and

understanding that your partner is a tremendous success, Divinely guided, Divinely expressed, and Divinely prospered in all ways, your beliefs will be conveyed to your partner subconsciously and your partner will fulfill your conviction of him or her. What you decree shall come to pass. Paul says: "Therefore, I put thee in remembrance that thou stir up the gift of God within thee."

10. Use the meditation at the end of the chapter to attain the peace and quiet of self-confidence.

17

How to Call Upon the Healing Presence to Bring the Riches You Want

Over ancient temples were written these words: *The doctor dresses the wound, but God heals the patient.* There is only one Universal Healing Power. It is omnipotent and omnipresent. It is in the stars and in the soil, in the cat, the dog, the elephant, and the worm. People call it by many names—God, Allah, the Over-Soul, Divine Providence, Nature, Cosmic Intelligence, and many others—but each name is simply a word that points our awareness toward the one Infinite Healing Presence.

This marvelous healing power resides in your own subconscious mind, which is the maker of your body. This healing power will heal a sick financial condition, a broken home, a disease-wracked body, marital discord, emotional distress, and troubles of all kinds. When you were young, you probably cut, scraped, and bruised yourself many times, and most of these times you probably ignored the hurt, confident in the knowledge that the healing process would take care of it. It is only as we grow in "wisdom" that we begin to lose this instinctive confidence in what some call the Wisdom of the Body.

How a Marriage Invoked the Riches of the Healing Presence

Daphne C. came to me in deep distress. In her midtwenties, she already had been promoted to a middle-management position with a major pharmaceutical company. There she had met and fallen in love with a brilliant young biochemist. They were now engaged to be married.

"My very best wishes," I said. "Why aren't you beaming with happiness?"

"It's my mother," she said in a choked voice. "I didn't tell you that Miguel is from Argentina. Not only that, his family is Jewish. And my mother . . . well, the nicest way to put it is that she's sort of old fashioned."

"You mean that she is prejudiced," I suggested. "She is not in favor of your marriage to Miguel because of his background and religion?"

Daphne burst into tears. I waited, then handed her a tissue. After a moment, she said, "I never knew she could be so hateful! She calls him names and says he's not fit for me. About the nicest thing she's said is to say he's a dirty foreigner!"

"Why do you think she is reacting this way?" I asked.

"Oh, I know why," she said bitterly. "She and my dad split up years ago, and she's dating this man—Don—who's like a total bigot. She's afraid if I get married to Miguel, Don will show her the door. Besides that, Don has this loser nephew Mom keeps trying to fix me up with. What can I say? She wants to totally run my life—and ruin it! I don't know if I can go on."

Alarmed, I asked, "What do you mean by that?"

She looked away. "I've started having these ideas . . . of getting away from it all. The pain, the fear . . . It would be such a comfort to just go to sleep and never wake up. I know these thoughts are unhealthy, even wicked, but I can't seem to make them go away. And I'm terribly afraid that in a weak moment, I might do something awful."

"Daphne," I said, "did you ever, when you were in the shower, pick up the bar of soap and feel it start to slip out of your hand?"

"Why, sure," she replied, with a startled look. "Why?"

"What usually happened then?"

"Well," she said, with a faint smile. "I'd squeeze harder, to keep from dropping it, and it would go shooting across the room!"

"Exactly," I said. "And right now, you're that bar of soap. Your mother feels you slipping away from her, so she squeezes tighter. But you know, deep inside yourself that you have to escape. That feeling is absolutely correct and Divinely inspired, but the only way to escape that occurs to you and causes such distress is not. You are here to develop, expand, and glorify your life, not to end it artificially."

"I feel that," she said, clasping her hands tightly. "But what can I do? I love Miguel. I don't care if he comes from a different country or a different religion. That doesn't matter a bit to me. I love him, and I want to marry him!"

"You're an adult," I pointed out. "You have the right and the duty to come to your own decision about who to spend your life with. And as you know in your deepest heart, love knows no creed, race, or color. Love transcends all these superficial categories. The minute you come to a decision to marry the man you love, a healing will come. These disturbing thoughts will go away forever."

Three weeks later, I performed the wedding ceremony for Daphne and Miguel. Afterwards, she telephoned her mother and told her she was married and on her way to a South American honeymoon. Her mother fumed, but Daphne said: "Mother, I have released you to God. You no longer dictate to me: neither do you manipulate my mind anymore. Good-bye and God bless you. From now on, I seek guidance from On High, and His wisdom and love will lead me into the ways of pleasantness and paths of peace."

Recently I had a letter from Daphne. She and her husband are now living in Buenos Aires, where they both work for the same pharmaceutical company. They are immensely happy and experiencing the riches of life. As for her mother, she later sought counsel from me and managed to develop a rapprochement with her daughter. Love pays fabulous dividends.

How to Apply the Healing Power of Freedom

"I'm terribly worried about my son, Arthur," Myrna B. told me. "He and his wife fight all the time, and I cannot approve of the way they are raising the kids. They're in their teens now and just running wild!"

"How old is your son?" I asked.

"Fifty-four last May," she replied.

"And you want a positive outcome in Divine order?" I continued.

"Of course I do. That's why I came to you," she said.

"Then the first thing you must understand is that you should never interfere in your son's marital problems," I said firmly. "Infinite Intelligence in him and his wife will deal with those. For your own good, you must stop thinking that he should do what you want him to do, or act the way you think he should act, or believe the way you think he should believe. You should release him, set him free, and get your own mind in order and at peace."

At the end of our consultation, I wrote out this prayer for her:

> I surrender my son, his wife, and family to God completely, lock, stock, and barrel. I loose them and let them go. I give him freedom to lead his own life in his own way, knowing that he is God's man and that God loves him and cares for him and his

family. I release him and set him free spiritually, mentally, and emotionally. Any time he, his wife, or his family come to my mind, I will immediately affirm, "I have released you. God be with you. I am free now and so are you." It is God in action in my life, which means harmony, peace, and right action.

She practiced this prayer therapy faithfully. Over the next few weeks, she found an inner sense of peace and tranquility that she had not known hitherto. She discovered a simple truth: When we set others free and release them to God's guidance and direction, we are set free ourselves.

Exalt the Divinity in your loved ones and friends and permit them to discover the Divinity that shapes their ends. Never try to bend them to your will or your own preconceived opinions and beliefs. Allow others to succeed or fail. If they fail, it may well be the turning point of their life, whereby they discover the power that never fails deep within themselves— the Infinite that lies stretched in smiling repose. In this way, you and they discover the riches of freedom.

How a Businessman Discovered the Riches of Surrender

"I want you to give me a prayer that'll bring my wife back," George W. told me. He was a vice president of a bank, but at this moment he was anything but cool and businesslike.

"Where did she go?" I inquired.

"I have no idea," he said. "Twenty years! Can you believe it? Happily married for 20 years, and one day I come back from a conference in Cleveland to find a note saying she was leaving me and getting a divorce! Incredible!"

"What do you expect this prayer you asked for to do?" I asked.

"I told you, get her back! She must be out of her mind, doing something like this. You give me a way to bring her back, and I'll bring her to her senses."

As we talked, I saw that George had been a very possessive and domineering husband who did not respect his wife's individuality. I explained to him that it is always wrong to try to force, mentally coerce, or try to influence another in any way to do one's bidding. He should not want a woman who didn't want him. He should grant her the right to make her own decisions, for what is Divine guidance for one is guidance for the other.

"You say she suddenly left with no reason," I continued. "That cannot be true. She must have been thinking of running away and visualizing life elsewhere for a long time. Finally, her mental image became solidified. Since the nature of the subconscious is compulsive, it caused her to pack up and leave. But she had been leaving mentally for a long time. When your body is in one place and in your imagination your mind is elsewhere, you will be eventually compelled to go where your vision is."

Love is not possessiveness. Love is not jealousy. Love is not domineering or coercive. When you love another, you love to see the other happy, joyous, and free. Love is freedom.

George listened closely to what I said. Finally he told me, "I still want a prayer, but I want one that will help bring about the best outcome, whatever that may be."

Accordingly, I gave him a pattern of prayer to follow:

> I surrender my wife to God completely. I know Infinite Intelligence leads and guides her in all ways. Divine right action reigns supreme. I know that what is right action for her is also right action for me. I give her complete freedom, because I know that love frees, it gives, it is the spirit of God. There are harmony, peace, and understanding between us. I wish for her all the blessings of life. I loose her and let her go.

He practiced this prayer therapy faithfully and with full inner consent. A few weeks later, he received a call from his wife. She told him she had filed for divorce and explained her reasons for leaving him in a loving, kind way. Both have since remarried, but they stay in touch.

Infinite Intelligence is all-wise. When you pray for guidance and right action, you do not tell the Infinite its business. George handled his crisis correctly, and the law of love gave him peace and tranquility. Love is the fulfilling of the law of health, happiness, prosperity, and peace of mind.

How a Nurse Received a Windfall of Money Through the Riches of the Healing Presence

On a flight to Mexico City, the woman in the next seat introduced herself as Nancy W. and told me she was a registered nurse. A New Yorker, she had been invited to teach in one of the biggest children's hospitals in Mexico. "I couldn't have accepted back when I was married," she said. "Now I'm looking forward to it as an adventure as well as a chance to give something back."

"You're divorced?" I asked.

"Uh-huh," she replied. "Mike and I were together five years. He was a psychiatric nurse. Then one day he asked for a divorce. He'd fallen for one of the staff at the hospital where he was working."

"That must have been difficult for you," I observed.

"Oh, yes, of course," Nancy said. "It was a shock. But I told Mike he was as free as the wind, that I wanted him to be happy. I belong to a metaphysical church in New York, and I know that love always frees. Mike was surprised that I wasn't angry or bitter, but I explained that true love is never possessive and added, 'By freeing you, I set myself free.' I don't think he quite got it, but he did appreciate it."

"I can understand that," I said. "And I can see that things worked out well for you. For him also?"

"I'm afraid not," she said, in a saddened tone. "His new marriage fell apart after a few months. Then last year, he suffered a fatal heart attack. I was flabbergasted to find out that I was the beneficiary of a very substantial life insurance policy. That's what allowed me to take on this teaching job. The hospital in Mexico can't afford to pay very much."

By setting her husband free and wishing for him all the blessings of life, Nancy had put her love and goodwill into practice, and it came back to her a hundred hundredfold.

How the Riches of the Healing Presence Worked for All in an Office

I was giving a series of lectures at San Diego's Royal Inn Hotel, overlooking the beautiful harbor full of ships from around the world, and I set aside a day for personal interviews. One of the first on the list was Judy L., a young woman fresh out of college who was in a trainee program at a brokerage firm.

"I love my job," Judy told me earnestly. "The work is fascinating, the pay is competitive, and the long-term prospects are excellent."

I smiled. "Is this what you consider a problem?" I asked.

"Well, no." She blushed. "The problem is most of the other trainees. I usually get along well with people, but they are so negative! They don't like the program, they don't like the pay, they don't like our bosses . . . I swear, if they won a million dollars in the lottery, they'd complain about the tax consequences! I feel bombarded by negative energy all day. By the time I leave in the evening, I am so depressed I'm dragging my chin on the sidewalk!"

"I have a suggestion," I said. I told her to write down the names of all the other trainees. Each morning before leaving for work and each evening after leaving she was to pray as follows:

All my coworkers are known in Divine mind. They are in their true place, doing what they love to do. They are Divinely happy and Divinely prospered. God thinks, speaks, and acts through them. They are conscious of their true worth and they are experiencing spiritual, mental, and material riches now. I loose them and let them go, and whenever I hear any negative statement from any one of them, I will immediately affirm, "God loves you and cares for you."

Over the next month, the most dissatisfied of the trainees left for positions in other fields. Those who stayed began to discover the gratifications in their work and brought a more positive attitude to the day. All of them were blessed. When the course finished and a new batch of trainees came in, Judy was asked to speak at their orientation. She found to her delight that they were all eager, positive, constructive thinkers and that several were students of the Science of Mind. Judy discovered that by blessing others, she not only contributed to their good, but also received the blessing back in great abundance.

How Parents Found the Riches of Releasing Their Daughter to a New Life

While in San Diego, I also met with Frank and Doris V. They were overwrought and emotionally wracked because their daughter, Ellen, had suddenly dropped out of college in the East and gone off to Hawaii with her boyfriend.

"Why did they go to Hawaii?" I asked.

"To become beach bums," Frank said bitterly. "What else?"

"Ellen's friend—they've known each other since high school—is a serious surfboarder," Doris interjected.

"As if there is such a thing," Frank said.

"Has Ellen been in touch with you?" I asked.

"Oh, yes, she's called twice," Doris said. "I was so relieved to hear her voice!"

"She wanted money," Frank added. "I'm supposed to send a money order to general delivery on Maui. Fat chance!"

"Now, Frank, you promised," Doris began.

I broke in to say, "Your daughter is an adult now. She has the right, and the duty, to live her own life without dictation from her parents. But beyond that, it is morally, ethically, and spiritually wrong to contribute to the laziness, apathy, and sloth of another person. It tends to turn them into leaners and whiners. If you get financial help too often and too easily, it robs you of your own initiative."

After much more discussion, Doris and Frank agreed to release their daughter completely. They were confident that the Infinite Healing Presence would take care of her in the right way, provided they used the law of mind in the right way.

The prayer therapy technique I outlined for them was as follows:

> I release my daughter to God completely. She is a daughter of God, and God loves her and cares for her. God is guiding her, and Divine law and order govern her entire life. Whenever we think of her, we will immediately affirm, "God is watching over you and He careth for you."

Over the next six weeks, they heard nothing from Ellen. They sent no money, but they prayed for her morning and night. On Tuesday of the seventh week, they received a letter from her. She was working in one of the big resort hotels and planned to enroll the following semester at the University of Hawaii and finish her degree. She apologized for what she had done and the pain she had caused them and asked forgiveness.

Doris phoned me that same day to say she and her husband were flying to Hawaii to see their child. I later got a postcard with the message that the reunion had been everything they could hope for. They had discovered the riches of releasing their daughter to the care of the Infinite, which knows all and sees all. Its ways are pleasantness and its paths are peace.

MEDITATION FOR APPLYING THE HEALING PRINCIPLE

I will restore health unto thee, and I will heal thee of thy wounds, saith the Lord. (Jeremiah 30:17) The God in me has limitless possibilities. I know that all things are possible with God. I believe this and accept it wholeheartedly now. I know that the God-Power in me makes darkness light and crooked things straight. I am now lifted up in consciousness by contemplating that God indwells me.

I speak the word now for the healing of mind, body, and affairs; I know that this Principle within me responds to my faith and trust. "The Father doeth the works." I am now in touch with life, love, truth, and beauty within me. I now align myself with the Infinite Principle of Love and Life within me. I know that harmony, health, and peace are now being expressed in my body.

As I live, move, and act in the assumption of my perfect health, it becomes actual. I now imagine and feel the reality of my perfect body. I am filled with a sense of peace and well-being. Thank you, Father.

☞ CHAPTER POINTS TO REMEMBER ☜

1. The Infinite Healing Presence is present everywhere. This Healing Presence heals a cut on your finger, reduces the edema in a burn, and restores your skin to a normal condition. It will also heal marital problems and financial troubles. It is the solution to all problems.

2. Parents should never interfere with the choice of a spouse selected by a daughter or son. The child should be free to make his or her own decision. The parents should simply release their offspring to God, knowing

that Infinite Intelligence guides and directs the young person, and that Divine right action prevails.

3. It is foolish to insist that your married sons or daughters should conform to your way of thinking, acting, and believing. Release your child to God, wishing for him all the blessings of life. Loose him and let him go. Where there is no opinion, there is no suffering. Whenever you think of a loved one, affirm: "I have released you. God be with you." When you do this, you set yourself free.

4. If your spouse packs up and leaves you, that is his or her decision. It is wrong to try to mentally coerce or force a partner to return. Use spiritual law by realizing Infinite Intelligence is guiding and directing him or her in all ways, knowing that what is Divine guidance for the other person is also guidance for you and for everybody in the world. Give the person Divine freedom, knowing that Divine right action prevails; then whatever happens blesses all. Love is not possessiveness. Love frees, it gives; it is the spirit of God.

5. Love always frees. Love is not possessiveness. When you love another, whether wife or husband, you love to see the other happy, joyous, and free. You love to see the other as the other ought to be. If your spouse falls madly in love with another, release her or him and wish for your spouse all the blessings of life. Love frees.

6. When others are talking negatively in your office, surrender all of them to God, knowing that God thinks, speaks, and acts through them and that they are Divinely led to their true expression in life. Radiate love, peace, and goodwill to them, and you will set the wonders of your prayer in action. They will be blessed, and so will you. You will discover that by exalting God in others, you also will bring countless blessings to yourself.

7. When your children are of age, loose them and let them go. Claim that God is guiding them and that they are in His care, and as you remain faithful to that prayer, your children will pick it up subjectively and be Divinely led to do the right thing. Be patient, trust the Infinite Intelligence within you, and don't argue in your mind. Infinite Intelligence knows all and sees all. All that is required of you is to trust and believe, and it is done unto you as you believe.

8. Apply the meditation at the end of the chapter for amazing benefits of the Healing Presence in your daily living.

How to Use Mind-Magic to Make Riches Flow

I once attended a religious convention at Airlie, near Washington, D.C., where I spoke on the topic, "The Law That Never Changes." During the five days I was there, I had a long talk with a very successful and immensely wealthy man named Peter L. He told me that the secret of his health, wealth, and outstanding achievement was in developing what he called the *quiet mind*.

He took a card from his pocket on which the following great truths were inscribed: *The superior man is always quiet and calm* (Confucius). *In quietness and in confidence shall be your strength* (Isaiah 30:15). *He that is slow to anger is better than the mighty; and he that ruleth his spirit than he that taketh a city* (Proverbs 16:32). *The Lord thy God shall bless thee in all thine increase, and in all the works of thine hands, therefore thou shalt surely rejoice* (Deuteronomy 16:15). *Except the Lord build the house, they labor in vain that build it* (Psalm 127:1).

All these statements point out that your strength, success, power, and riches come from serenity, from the inner peace of quietness, and from confidence in the laws of life and the response of your subconscious mind.

How This Rich Man Used These Truths

Peter said that every morning of his life he anchored his mind on the aforementioned truths, repeating them slowly, quietly, and lovingly. He knew that as they were impressed in his subconscious mind, he would be compelled to express success, health, vitality, and new creative ideas. He is the founder of a major corporation, a board member of half a dozen more, and a trusted adviser to many executives in different fields. He travels the world over.

As he gave me one of his meditation cards, which he dispenses freely to those he meets, he told me that 30 years ago, on a ship to Europe, he met a man who changed his life. This man explained to him that if he took certain constructive words from the Bible—words that represent the eternal truths of God and His Law—his mind would become anchored on the Supreme Presence, which responds as you call upon It.

The whole key to Peter's riches is that he knew as he meditated on the aforementioned biblical phrases regularly, systematically, and repetitiously, he was activating the latent power within his subliminal depths, compelling him to move onward, upward, and Godward.

A Business Executive Discovers the Riches of Silence

The philosopher Thomas Carlyle said, "Silence is the element in which great things fashion themselves." Emerson said, "Let us be silent that we may hear the whispers of the gods."

These sentences are engraved on a cherrywood plaque that hangs in the office of Eleanor A., the executive vice president of a Fortune 500 media conglomerate. During an interview, I noticed and remarked on them.

"I attribute all my success to those great thoughts," Eleanor told me. "Every morning before work, I meditate for 15 minutes. I withdraw my attention and sensory awareness from the external world, quiet my body, close my eyes, and contemplate the great truth that Infinite Intelligence is within me and each of us."

She added that she makes a silent affirmation that God is guiding her; that new, creative ideas are given to her; that the Divine Presence will govern the conferences of the day; that God thinks, speaks, and acts through her; that the right words are given to her by the Supreme Wisdom within her; and that all decisions for her company are based on right action, blessing all.

She then spends about five minutes imagining God's river of peace flowing through her whole being. Often, while in this quiet period, solutions to difficult business and personnel problems pop into her mind, problems with which she and her associates have been struggling for days.

How to Get the Answers

"I've discovered that the quickest way in the world to get the answer to a problem is to turn over your request to that center of quietness, " Eleanor remarked later in our conversation. "I know the answer will emerge. Sometimes it comes right away or within an hour. Other times, it may take a few days or even a week, but it always comes. The strange part is that it usually comes when I am preoccupied with something else. I guess my subconscious mind gathers all the material necessary and then, at the right time, presents it full-blown to my conscious, reasoning mind."

Some of the answers that have come to her in this way have been immensely valuable. One recent idea that emerged from her quiet period led to a new business strategy that increased the company's market valuation by millions of dollars.

How a Quiet Mind Dissolved Destructive Criticism

Doug H. was recently promoted to head of his department in a service-sector corporation. Because he is younger and newer to the firm than many of the people he is now supervising, he has been the target of a good deal of criticism and backbiting.

"You seem very calm saying that," I remarked when he told me. "How do you handle the situation?"

"I try to take it philosophically," he replied. "I remind myself of the words of the Bible, *When he giveth quietness, who then can make trouble?* (Job 34:29). I link up with the God-Presence within me and know that no one can hurt me, as 'one with God is a majority.' In any case, I know that the negative thoughts and statements of others have no power to create the things they suggest unless I transfer the power within me to them. And I refuse to do that. My thought is creative. My thoughts are God's thoughts, and God's power is with my thoughts of good."

Doug is a wise young man who is clearly destined for great things. He knows that no matter what lies others may spread about him, they cannot hurt him unless he accepts the thought mentally. Because others speak ill of you does not make it so. Your thought is creative, and you are the master of your own mind. You must positively refuse to let others disturb you or manipulate your mind.

There is an old German proverb: "A lie cannot go very far, for it has short legs."

How an Anxious Manager Discovered the Riches of Healing Passages of the Bible

Recently I was consulted by Stephen J., a manager, who told me, "My problem is anxiety. I suffer torments over every decision I have to make." Accordingly, I gave him what I call a spiritual prescription to bring peace to his troubled mind. I suggested to him that if he affirmed the following spiritual truths quietly, feelingly, and knowingly, his excess tension would gradually abate:

Thou wilt keep him in perfect peace, whose mind is stayed on thee, because he trusteth in thee (Isaiah 26:3). *In quietness and confidence shall be your strength* (Isaiah 30:15). *But my God shall supply all your need according to his riches in glory* (Philippians 4:19). *Acquaint now thyself with him, and be at peace: thereby good shall come unto thee* (Job 22:21). *Casting all your care upon him; for he careth for you* (I Peter 5:7). *When he giveth quietness, who then can make trouble?* (Job 34:29).

When this manager affirmed these healing, therapeutic passages of scripture several times daily, spending five or ten minutes at each quiet session, he found composure, peace, serenity, and mind control. He discovered that peace is the power at the heart of God.

A Sales Rep Discovers the Secret of Increased Sales in the Riches of a Quiet Mind

Bettina B. was a sales representative for a manufacturer of paper goods. She came to me very worried about a letter she had recently received from her supervisor. This criticized her for what he regarded as low productivity and implied that she might lose her job if she didn't improve soon.

I suggested to her that she read the 23rd Psalm night and morning to quiet her mind, then put the faculty of using her imagination constructively to work. Imagination is the art or discipline of projecting mental images in a productive way.

Under my guidance, Bettina reversed the mental image she had harbored of poor sales and failure. Morning and night for five or ten minutes, after reading out loud the 23rd Psalm, she imagined her sales manager coming out from his office to congratulate her publicly on her excellent sales. She felt the naturalness of his handshake. She clearly saw his smile and heard him say, "Congratulations on your splendid performance. You are being promoted." She lulled herself to sleep every night while watching this mental movie.

Bettina's sales soon improved. At the end of three months, she was made district manager, receiving a wonderful increase in salary and commissions. She is on the way to the top. By repeating the mental movie night and morning in a quiet, passive, receptive way, she implanted the idea of promotion and advancement in her subconscious mind, which opened the way for the perfect manifestation of the impression she had made.

How the Riches of Quiet Understanding Healed a Threatened Mental Crack-Up

Mark A. flew down from San Francisco to see me. He was extremely tense. His doctor had diagnosed his condition as anxiety neurosis, which is another name for chronic worry and excess tension. He was financially successful and was sales manager of a very big corporation. He was well liked by the president and vice president of the corporation.

As I talked with him, the root cause of his trouble came to light. A classmate of his was an executive with a rival corporation and had recently been selected as CEO. "I can't stand it!" Mark exclaimed. "That guy came out ahead of me at everything in college. He beat me for the presidency of our fraternity. He even took away the girl I loved and married her. And now this!"

I explained to Mark that the only true competition in life was between the idea of success and the idea of failure in his own mind. He was born to win, not fail, for the Infinite cannot fail. Once he focused his attention on success, all the powers of his subconscious would back him up and compel him to succeed, as the law of the subconscious is compulsive.

He began to realize that the past is dead and that nothing matters but this moment. By entertaining envious thoughts, he was actually impoverishing himself. This was one of the worst possible attitudes to hold, because his negative thinking and his feeling of inferiority plus envy and jealousy were playing havoc with his mental and emotional life and would tend to block his expansion along all lines.

The Simple Remedy

The remedy was simple. Mark decided to bless and sincerely wish greater prosperity and success for his former classmate, whose success had incited him to envy. Accordingly, he prayed frequently as follows:

> I recognize God as my instant and everlasting supply. Promotion is mine in Divine order. Success is mine in Divine order. God's wealth flows to me in avalanches of abundance, and I am Divinely guided to give better service every day. I know, believe, and rejoice that God is prospering my former classmate, and I sincerely wish for him all the blessings of life. Whenever he comes to my mind, I will immediately affirm, God multiplies your good.

After a few weeks, he discovered that the envious thoughts lost all momentum, and he found that the cause of his anxiety and excess tension had been due entirely to his state of mind. Mark was recently promoted to executive vice president and undoubtedly is on the way to the top. The Bible says: *If thou return to the Almighty, thou shalt be built up* (Job 22:23).

By blessing those whose promotion, success, and wealth annoy us or incite our envy or jealousy and by wishing that they become even more prosperous and more successful in every way, we heal our own minds and open the door to the riches of the Infinite. Out of the abundance of your heart you can pour out the gifts of praise, love, joy, and laughter. You can give a transfusion of courage, faith, and confidence to all those around you, and you will discover that by blessing others, you, too, will be blessed, and all sense of envy, inferiority, and lack will be overcome.

A Medical Student Discovers the Riches of the Quiet Mind

Alice R., a fourth-year medical student, said to me, "I'm haunted by a shadowy, pervasive anxiety day and night, a sense of failure and apprehension about the future." She said that in one examination her mind went blank and she could answer only a few of the questions. Alice's trouble was anxiety and worry. She was afraid of oral and written examinations and was giving the worry orders to her subconscious mind. She developed stress, which brought about a mental block.

I suggested that every night prior to sleep, she should affirm slowly and quietly,

> I am relaxed, at peace, serene, and calm. I have a perfect memory for everything I need to know at every moment of time and point of space. I am Divinely guided in my studies and I am completely relaxed and at peace at all examinations. I pass all my examinations in Divine order, and I sleep in peace and I wake in joy.

I explained to her that all these ideas would sink deeply into her subconscious mind, becoming a part of her, so that either in an oral or a written examination she would give an excellent account of herself.

At last report, Alice is doing splendidly. Her anxiety has been lifted, and her latent abilities and memory of all she learned were set free. *In quietness and in confidence shall be your strength* (Isaiah 30:15).

MEDITATION FOR THE RICHES OF THE QUIET MIND

The following meditation repeated often can bring you your heart's desires in unexpected ways:

> *Those that be planted in the house of the Lord shall flourish in the courts of our God.* (Psalms 92:13) I am still and at peace. My heart and my mind are motivated by the spirit of goodness, truth, and beauty. My thought is now on the presence of God within me; this stills my mind.
>
> I know that the way of creation is Spirit moving upon itself. My True Self now moves in and on itself creating peace, harmony, and health in my body and affairs. I am Divine in my deeper self. I know I am a child of the living God; I create the way God creates by the self-contemplation of spirit. I know my body does not move of itself. It is acted upon by my thoughts and emotions.
>
> I now say to my body, "Be still and quiet." It must obey. I understand this and I know it is a Divine law. I take my attention away from the physical world; I feast in the house of God within me. I meditate and feast upon harmony, health, and peace; these come forth from the God-Essence within; I am at peace. My body is a temple of the Living God. *The Lord is in His Holy Temple; let all the earth keep silence before Him.* (Habakkuk 2:20)

☞ CHAPTER POINTS TO REMEMBER ☞

1. Confucius said: "The superior man is always quiet and calm." The Bible says: *In quietness and in confidence shall be your strength* (Isaiah 30:15). The secret of health,

wealth, and outstanding achievement is in developing what is called the "quiet mind." By taking certain constructive words from the Bible, which represent the eternal truths of God and His Law, your mind becomes anchored on the Supreme Presence, which responds as you call upon it, and you experience the riches of the quiet mind.

2. Carlyle said: "Silence is the element in which great things fashion themselves." Emerson said: "Let us be silent that we may hear the whispers of the gods." Silently affirm that God is guiding you, that the Divine wisdom will govern all your activities of the day, and that God thinks, speaks, and acts through you every day. Claim Divine right action in all your undertakings. Practice meditation by imagining God's river of peace and love flowing through your whole being. As you do this, you will receive answers to all your problems welling up from the depths of yourself, and wonders will happen in your life.

3. When you quiet your mind and immobilize your attention, realize only God knows the answer. Contemplate the answer, the solution, knowing that before you call, the answer is known to your Higher Self. You will discover there are creative answers in your subconscious that will revolutionize your life

4. *When he giveth quietness, who then can make trouble?* (Job 34:29). The suggestions, statements, and actions of others cannot hurt you. The creative power is in you—it is the movement of your own thought. Does another person's thought govern you, or do you govern your own mind? When your thoughts are God's thoughts, God's power is with your thoughts of good.

5. If you have difficulty sleeping, talk to your body, telling it to relax, let go. Your body will obey you and then

affirm slowly and quietly, "I sleep in peace and I wake in joy, for He careth for me."

6. You can eradicate excess tension and anxiety by affirming the following spiritual truths three or four times daily: *Thou wilt keep him in perfect peace, whose mind is stayed on thee: because he trusteth in thee* (Isaiah 26:3). *In quietness and confidence shall be your strength* (Isaiah 30:15). *Acquaint now thyself with him, and be at peace: thereby good shall come unto thee* (Job 22:21). *When he giveth quietness, who then can make trouble?* (Job 34:29). As you dwell on these great biblical truths, a healing, therapeutic vibration permeates your entire body. These spiritual vibrations enter into your subconscious mind, neutralizing all fear and worry patterns. A sense of peace and tranquility will govern you.

7. A sales rep whose sales were dropping imagined her sales manager congratulating her on her excellent sales. By repetition she implanted the idea of promotion in her subconscious mind and eventually experienced a wonderful promotion and increase in salary.

8. The only place competition takes place is in your own mind; the idea of success and the thought of failure compete. You were born to succeed, not to fail. The Infinite within you can't fail. Give your attention to the idea of success and all the powers of your deeper mind will back you up. Prayer always prospers.

9. A medical student was fearful and apprehensive about her examinations. Actually, she was fearing failure. This develops stress, which blocks the mind. She affirmed prior to sleep: "I am relaxed, at peace, poised, serene, and calm. I have a perfect memory for everything I need to know at all times everywhere. I pass all examinations in Divine order. I sleep in peace and I wake in joy." These truths sank into her subconscious mind and she is

now doing splendidly. She discovered the riches of the truth: *In quietness and confidence shall be your strength* (Isaiah 30:15).

10. You can experience the benefits of quieting the mind through using the meditation at the end of the chapter.

How to Start Living Like a King—Almost Overnight

The Bible says: *I am come that they might have life, and that they might have it more abundantly* (John 10:10). Johann Goethe said: "Life is a quarry, out of which we are to mold and chisel and complete a character."

You are here to lead a full, joyous, successful, and rich life along all lines. You were born to win, to conquer, and to triumph over all obstacles. You are here to release your wonderful hidden talents, to bless mankind, and to express yourself at the highest possible level. Call upon Infinite Intelligence within you to reveal to you your true place in life. Follow the lead that comes clearly and distinctly into your conscious, reasoning mind. When you find your true expression in life, you will be perfectly happy. Health, wealth, and all the other blessings of life will follow.

Your success and prosperity in the art of living a wonderful and glorious life depend on your habitual thinking and your heart's desire to transform your life from top to bottom. Remember, you go where your vision is. What is your vision? It is that about which you think, that to which you direct your attention, the object upon which you are focused. Whatever you give attention to, your subconscious will magnify and multiply exceedingly in your life.

Accept Wealth
and Happiness Now

Now is the time. I talk to many people who are constantly looking forward to better times somewhere down the road. Many believe that some day they will be happy, prosperous, and successful. Some are waiting for their children to grow up; then they say they will travel to Europe and Asia and see the many strange, faraway places. Others talk about how they plan to spend their retirement years.

All these people are waiting for something to happen, instead of realizing that God is the Eternal Now—their good is now, this moment, waiting for them to claim it. As you have seen demonstrated in this book by now, you are in command now for a full, prosperous life.

One man said that someday he would hit the jackpot and make his mark on the world. His wife said that she hoped someday she would finally cure a painful skin rash. I explained to both of them that all the powers of God were within each of them. Peace is now. You can claim God's river of peace flows through you now. The Infinite Healing Presence is available, and you can claim that this Healing Presence is flowing through you now, making you whole, pure, and perfect.

It dawned on the husband and wife that wealth and healing are available now. The woman began to affirm night and morning as follows: "God's Healing Presence is saturating my whole being and Divine Love flows through my whole being. My skin is an envelope of God's love and is whole, pure, and perfect, without spot or blemish."

Within one week, she proved to herself that the Infinite Healing was instantly available to her, and she had a complete healing.

I explained to her husband that wealth is available now, that it is a thought-image in the mind. He began to affirm boldly:

"God's wealth is now circulating in my life. I am engraving this idea in my subconscious mind, and I know that whatever I impress on my subconscious mind will come to pass. I realize as I continue to do this that the response from my subconscious mind will be compulsive, and I will be compelled to express wealth."

As he continued praying in this manner, new creative ideas welled up within him. He made canny investments in oil stocks, both foreign and domestic, and in a matter of months he had earned a small fortune. He had a preponderant feeling, a sort of persistent intuitive urge to buy these stocks, all of which soared greatly in value immediately. He proved to himself that wealth was available here and now.

Claim Your Spiritual, Mental, and Material Riches Now

Strength is now. Call on the Infinite Power of God within you and this power will respond, energizing, vitalizing, and renewing your whole being now. Love is now. Claim that God's love envelops and saturates your mind and body. Realize and know that Divine Love is being filtered through you and manifested in all phases of your life. Guidance is now. Infinite Intelligence responds to your call. It knows only the answer and will reveal it to you now. Claim your good now. You do not create anything; all you do is to give form and expression to that which always was, now is, and ever shall be.

Plan for a Rich Future Now

Remember that if you are planning something in the future, you are planning it now. If you are worried about the future, you are fearing it now. If you are dwelling on the past, you are thinking of it now. You have control over your present thoughts. All you have to change are your present thoughts and keep them changed. You are aware of your present thoughts. All that you can realize is the outer manifestation of your habitual thinking at the present moment.

Beware of the Two Thieves Stealing from You

The "past" and the "future" are the two arch thieves. If you are indulging in remorse and self-criticism over past mistakes and hurts, the mental agony you experience is the pain of your present thought. If you are fearful about the future, you are robbing and stealing from yourself joy, health, happiness, and peace of mind. Begin to count your blessings now and get rid of the two thieves.

To think of a happy and joyful episode in the past is a present joy. Remember, the results of past events—good or bad—are but the representation of your present thinking. Direct your present thoughts into the right channels. Enthrone in your mind peace, harmony, joy, love, prosperity, and good will. Dwell consciously and frequently on these concepts and claim them and forget all other things.

Finally, brethren, whatsoever things are true, whatsoever things are honest, whatsoever things are just, whatsoever things are pure, whatsoever things are lovely, whatsoever things are of good report; if there be any virtue, and if there be any praise, think on these things (Philippians 4:8).

Take this spiritual medicine regularly and systematically and you will build a glorious future.

MEDITATION FOR MIRACLE POWER STEPS TO RICHER LIVING AND FINANCIAL SUCCESS

It will pay you great dividends to use this meditation as often as possible:

Wist ye not that I be about my Father's business. (Luke 2:49) I know that my business, profession, or activity is God's business. God's business is always basically successful. I am growing in wisdom and understanding every day. I know, believe, and accept the fact that God's law of abundance is always working for me, through me, and all around me.

My business or profession is full of right action and right expression. The ideas, money, merchandise, and contacts I need are mine now and at all times. All these things are irresistibly attracted to me by the law of universal attraction. God is the life of my business; I am Divinely guided and inspired in all ways. Every day I am presented with wonderful opportunities to grow, expand, and progress. I am building up goodwill. I am a great success, because I do business with others as I would have them do it with me.

↩ CHAPTER POINTS TO REMEMBER ↪

1. You are here to lead the abundant life, a life full of love, peace, joy, and rich living. Begin now to release the riches of the treasure house within you.

2. You go where your vision is. Whatever you give attention to, your subconscious will magnify and multiply in your experience.

3. Accept your wealth, health, and success now. Stop procrastinating. God is the Eternal Now. This means your good is now. Claim peace now. Claim that God's love fills your soul now, this minute. Wealth is a thought-image in your mind. Claim that God's wealth is circulating in your life now. As you make a habit of this, your subconscious will compel you to express wealth.

4. Claim all your good now. Remember, you do not really create anything; all you do is give form and expression to that which always was, now is, and ever shall be.

5. Plan a rich and glorious future now. If you are planning something in the future, you are planning it now. If you are thinking about the past, you are thinking about it now. You can control the present moment. Change your present thought-pattern to conform to health, wealth, and success, and your future is certain. Your future is your present thought-pattern made manifest

6. Beware of the two thieves. If you are indulging in remorse over past mistakes or are worrying about the future, you should be aware that these two thieves rob you of vitality, discernment, and peace of mind.

7. Use the meditation at the end of the chapter as your faultless guide in taking the miracle power steps to richer living and financial success.

Index